ACI DEALING CERTIFICATE EXAM PRACTICE QUESTIONS & DUMPS

440+ EXAM PRACTICE QUESTIONS FOR ACI DEALING Certificate UPDATED 2020

Presented By: Librito Books

Copyright © 2020 by Librito Books

All rights reserved. No part of this publication may be reproduced, distributed, or transmitted in any form or by any means, including photocopying, recording, or other electronic or mechanical methods, without the prior written permission of the publisher, except in the case of brief quotations embodied in critical reviews and certain other noncommercial uses permitted by copyright law.

First Copy Printed in 2020

About Librito Books:

Librito Books is a publishing house based in US, a platform that is available both online & locally, which unleashes the power of educational content, literary collection, poetry & many other book genres. We make it easy for writers & authors to get their books designed, published, promoted, and sell professionally on worldwide scale with eBook + Print distribution. Librito Books was founded in 2016, and is now distributing books worldwide.

Sections

1. Volume A
2. Volume B
3. Volume C
4. Volume D
5. Volume E
6. Volume F
7. Volume G

Exam A

QUESTION 1

You are quoted the following market rates: spot USD/SEK 6.3850
1M (30-day) USD 0.40%
1M (30-day) SEK 1.15%

What is 1-month USD/SEK?
A. 6.4250
B. 6.3810
C. 6.7850
D. 6.3890

Correct Answer: D Section: Volume A

QUESTION 2

You are quoted the following market rates: Spot GBP/USD 1.5525
9M (272-day) GBP 0.81%
9M (272-day) USD 0.55%

What are the 9-month GBP/USD forward points? A. -30
B. +29
C. -29
D. +30

Correct Answer: C Section: Volume A

QUESTION 3

You quote a customer spot AUD/USD at 1.0350-55. The T/N swap is quoted to you at 3/2. The customer asks to buy USD for value tomorrow. What rate should you quote him to break-even against the other rates?

A. 1.0352
B. 1.0353
C. 1.0347
D. 1.0348

Correct Answer: A Section: Volume A

QUESTION 4

Which of the following is true about interest rate swaps (IRS):

A. Both parties know what their future payments will be at the outset of the swap
B. There is payment of principal at maturity
C. Payments are always made gross
D. The fixed rate payer knows what his future payments will be at the outset of the swap

Correct Answer: D Section: Volume A

QUESTION 5

Which of the following is true?

A. The 3-month Sterling (SHORT STERLING) futures contract has a basis point value of GBP 25.00 and a face value of GBP 1,000,000 .00
B. The EUROYEN TIBOR futures contract has a basis point value of JPY 25,000 and a face value of JPY 1,000,000,000
C. The CME EURODOLLAR futures contract has a minimum price interval of one-quarter basis point value (0.0025) for the nearest contract
D. The 3-month EURIBOR futures contract has a minimum price interval of half a basis point value (0.0050) for the nearest contract

Correct Answer: C Section: Volume A

QUESTION 6

EURODOLLAR futures are:

A. Traded on the Chicago Mercantile Exchange (CME Group) and have a face value of USD 500,000.00
B. Traded on the Intercontinental Exchange (ICE) and have a face value of USD 1,000,000.00
C. Traded on the Intercontinental Exchange (ICE) and have a face value of USD 500,000.00
D. Traded on the Chicago Mercantile Exchange (CME Group) and have a face value of USD 1,000,000.00

Correct Answer: D Section: Volume A

QUESTION 7

You have a short position of 50 EURODOLLAR futures contracts. You can hedge your position by:

A. Selling a FRA for a similar notional amount
B. Buying a FRA for a similar notional amount
C. Selling a call option on the contract
D. Selling a put option on the contract
E.

Correct Answer: A Section: Volume A

QUESTION 8

If a dealer has a 6-month USD asset and a 3-month USD liability, how could he hedge his balance sheet exposure in the FRA market?

A. Buy 3x6
B. Sell 3x6
C. Buy 0x6
D. Sell 6x9

Correct Answer: A Section: Volume A

QUESTION 9

What is the Overnight Index for EUR?

A. EURIBOR
B. EONIA
C. EUREPO
D. EURONIA

Correct Answer: B Section: Volume A

QUESTION 10

You bought a CAD 8,000,000.00 6x9 FRA at 1.95%. The settlement rate is 3-month (90-day) BBA LIBOR, which is fixed at 0.9500%. What is the settlement amount at maturity?

A. You pay CAD 20,000.00
B. You receive CAD 20,000.00
C. You pay CAD 19,952.61
D. You receive CAD 19,952.61

Correct Answer: C Section: Volume A

QUESTION 11

Which of the following is true?

A. The 3-month EURODOLLAR futures contract has a basis point value of USD 50.00 and a face value of USD 1,000,000.00
B. The 3-month EURIBOR futures contract has a a basis point value of EUR 12.50 and a face value of EUR 500,000.00
C. The 3-month Sterling (SHORT STERLING) futures contract has a a basis point value of GBP 12.50 and a face value of GBP 500,000.00
D. The 3-month Euro Swiss Franc (EUROSWISS) futures contract has a a basis point value of CHF 50.00 and a face value of CHF 2,000,000.00

Correct Answer: C Section: Volume A

QUESTION 12

Basis risk on a futures contract is:

A. The risk of an adverse change in the futures price
B. The risk of an adverse change in the spread between futures and cash prices
C. The progressive illiquidity of a futures contract as it approaches expiry
D. The risk of a divergence between the futures price and the final fixing of the underlying interest rate

Correct Answer: B Section: Volume A

QUESTION 13

Lending for 3 months and borrowing for 6 months creates a 3x6 forward-forward deposit. The cost of that deposit is called:

A. Implicit nominal rate
B. Implied forward rate
C. Funding rate
D. Effective future rate

Correct Answer: B Section: Volume A

QUESTION 14

A corporate wishing to hedge the interest rate risk on its floating-rate borrowing would:

A. Sell interest rate caps
B. Sell futures
C. Sell FRAs
D. Buy futures

Correct Answer: B Section: Volume A

QUESTION 15

The market is quoting:

6-month (182-day) CAD 1.25% 12-month (366-day) CAD 1.55%

What is the 6x12 rate in CAD? A. 0.300%
B. 0.946%
C. 1.935%
D. 1.835%
Correct Answer: D Section: Volume A
QUESTION 16

The seller of a put option has:

A. Substantial opportunity for gain and limited risk of loss
B. Substantial risk of loss and substantial opportunity for gain
C. Limited risk of loss and limited opportunity for gain
D. Substantial risk of loss and limited opportunity for gain

Correct Answer: D

Section: Volume A

QUESTION 17

The exercise price in an option contract is:

A. The price of the underlying instrument at the time of the transaction
B. The price at which the transaction on the underlying instrument will be carried out if and when the option is exercised
C. The price the buyer of the option pays to the seller when entering into the options contract
D. The price at which the two counterparties can close-out their position

Correct Answer: B **Section: Volume A**

QUESTION 18

An 'at-the-money' option has:

A. Intrinsic value but no time value
B. Time value but no intrinsic value
C. Both time value and intrinsic value
D. Neither time value nor intrinsic value

Correct Answer: B **Section: Volume A**

QUESTION 19

The vega of an option is:

A. The sensitivity of the option value to changes in interest rates
B. The sensitivity of the option value to changes in implied volatility
C. The sensitivity of the option value to changes in the time to expiry
D. The sensitivity of the option value to changes in the price of the underlying

Correct Answer: B **Section: Volume A**

QUESTION 20
An option is:

A. The right to buy or sell a commodity at a fixed price
B. The right to buy a commodity at a fixed price
C. The right but not the obligation to buy or sell a commodity at a fixed price
D. The right but not the obligation to buy a commodity at a fixed price

Correct Answer: C Section: Volume A

QUESTION 21
A put option is 'out-of-the-money' if:

A. Its strike price is higher than the current market price of the underlying commodity
B. If the current market price of the underlying commodity is higher than the strike price of the option
C. Its strike price is equal to the current market price of the underlying commodity
D. If the current market price of the underlying commodity is lower than the strike price of the option

Correct Answer: B Section: Volume A

QUESTION 22
Which of the following transactions would have the effect of lengthening the average duration of assets in the banking book?

A. buying futures contracts on 30-year German Government bonds
B. selling futures contracts on 30-year German Government bonds
C. buying put options on 30-year German Government bonds
D. buying a 3x6 forward rate agreement

Correct Answer: A Section: Volume A

QUESTION 23
What is a 'duration gap'?

A. the average maturity of liabilities on a balance sheet
B. the difference between the duration of assets and liabilities
C. the difference between the duration of the longest-held and shortest-held liabilities on the balance sheet
D. the average maturity of the portfolio on the asset side of a balance sheet

Correct Answer: B Section: Volume A

QUESTION 24
Which statement about modern matched-maturity transfer pricing in banks is correct?

A. It is now a widely accepted standard that banks should use a single representative transfer price across the entire maturity spectrum.
B. Modern matched-maturity pricing systems include an additional liquidity surcharge that is specifically applied to more liquid short maturities.
C. Matched-maturity transfer prices should represent a weighted average cost of capital that incorporates the cost of equity into the cost of borrowed funds.
D. Modern matched-maturity systems differentiate transfer prices by the maturity of the commitment and also apply a marginal funding cost perspective.

Correct Answer: D Section: Volume A

QUESTION 25
Supervisors would generally consider interest rate risk exposure in the banking book excessive beginning at what level of losses given a +1- 200 bps market rate movement?

A. > 2% of 6 months forward earnings
B. > 20% of regulatory capital
C. <10% of regulatory capital
D. < 5% of 12 months forward earnings

Correct Answer: B Section: Volume A

QUESTION 26
Which one of the following statements is incorrect? Hedge accounting of an existing position no longer applies when:

A. The trader acquires additional exposure in the hedged item.
B. The hedging instrument is sold, terminated or exercised.
C. The hedged item is sold or settled.
D. A hedge fails the effectiveness test.

Correct Answer: A Section: Volume A

QUESTION 27
Which of the following is a function of asset and liability management (ALM)?

A. coordinated limit management of a financial institution's credit portfolio
B. running a matched trading book
C. monitoring credit quality of assets and establishing a early warning system
D. managing the financial risk of the bank by protecting it from the adverse effects of changing interest rates

Correct Answer: B Section: Volume A

QUESTION 28
Which of the following statements is correct?

A. Unilateral collateral obligations to sovereign counterparties provide liquidity to banks.
B. Under Basel III commercial banks are most likely to incur lower costs to service their sovereign clients.
C. While banks usually do not call for collateral from sovereign counterparties, they must provide collateral for the offsetting hedge transactions which are undertaken with commercial counterparties.
D. Uncollateralised exposures to sovereign counterparties will not require additional regulatory capital to be set aside against potential credit losses

Correct Answer: C Section: Volume A

QUESTION 29
Which one of the following statements about interest rate movements is true?

A. An upward parallel shift of interest rates will cause a loss of income if the rate-sensitivity of a bank's liabilities is higher than the rate-sensitivity of its assets.
B. A bank will lose income if it has more rate-sensitive liabilities than rate-sensitive assets.
C. Falling interest rates will always result in mark-to-market profits on short positions in fixed rate securities.
D. Rising interest rates can result in mark-to-market losses on fixed-rate assets.

Correct Answer: D Section: Volume A

QUESTION 30
Under Basel rules, what is the meaning of EEPE?

A. Effective Expected Potential Exposure
B. Effective Expected Positive Exposure
C. Effective Expected Price Earning
D. Effective Expected Payment Exposure

Correct Answer: B Section: Volume A

QUESTION 31
The major risk to the effectiveness of netting is:

A. Credit risk
B. Settlement risk
C. Liquidity risk
D. Legal risk

Correct Answer: D Section: Volume A

QUESTION 32
Which of the following methods is a means of credit risk mitigation?

A. entering into a plain vanilla IRS
B. entering into collateral agreements
C. hedging a portfolio's USD exposure
D. investing only in sizeable and liquid markets

Correct Answer: B Section: Volume A

QUESTION 33
Which of the following scenarios offer an example of wrong way risk?

A. A bank purchases credit protection on highly-rated tranches of US mortgage-backed securities from a US mortgage bank
B. A bank sells protection on the iTraxx main index at a level of 25 bps and shortly afterwards the index crosses the 200 bps level
C. A bank sells EUR put I USD call ATM options with an expiry date of 6 months and afterwards volatility moves up to substantially higher levels
D. A bank enters into a receiver's swap while interest rates are increasing

Correct Answer: A Section: Volume A

QUESTION 34
Which of the following is typical of liquid assets held by banks under prudential requirements?

A. prices increase during a systemic crisis
B. return on investment is relatively high
C. absence of active market makers
D. wide bid/offer spreads

Correct Answer: A Section: Volume A

QUESTION 35
What is the correct interpretation of a EUR 2,000,000.00 overnight VaR figure with a 97% confidence level?

A. A loss of at least EUR 2,000,000.00 can be expected in 97 out of the next 100 days.
B. A loss of at most EUR 2,000,000.00 can be expected in 3 out of the next 100 days.
C. A loss of at least EUR 2,000,000.00 can be expected in 3 out of the next 100 days.
D. A loss of at most EUR 2,000,000.00 can be expected in 6 out of the next 100 days.

Correct Answer: C Section: Volume A

QUESTION 36
Hybex Electrics is a highly rated company with a considerable amount of fixed rate liabilities and would like to increase the percentage of floating rate debt. Which of the following is the best course of action?

A. Hybex should become a payer of a fixed rate on a swap against receipt of LIBOR.
B. Hybex should become a receiver of a floating rate on a swap against payment of a fixed rate
C. Hybex should become a receiver of a fixed rate on a swap against payment of LIBOR D.
D. Hybex should become a receiver of a floating rate on a swap against payment of LIBOR

Correct Answer: C Section: Volume A

QUESTION 37
Which one of the following statements correctly describes the increased capital ratios that will come into effect under Basel III?

A. minimum tier 1 capital of 4.5% and minimum total capital plus a conservation buffer of 10.5%
B. minimum tier 1 capital of 6% and minimum total capital including conservation buffer of 8%
C. minimum tier 1 capital of 4% and minimum total capital including conservation buffer of 10.5%
D. minimum tier 1 capital of 6% and minimum total capital including conservation buffer of 10.5%

Correct Answer: D Section: Volume A

QUESTION 38
Responsibility for the activities of all personnel engaged in dealing (both dealers and support staff) for both principals and brokers lies with:

A. the market supervisor
B. the national ACI association
C. the management of such organizations
D. the central bank

Correct Answer: C Section: Volume A

QUESTION 39
Which Greek letter is used to describe the ratio of change in the option price compared with change in the price of the underlying instrument, when all other conditions are fixed?

A. beta
B. gamma
C. delta
D. theta

Correct Answer: C Section: Volume A

QUESTION 40
When banks transact FX swaps, the spot price should be determined:

A. anytime after the swap is transacted
B. before the swap is transacted
C. immediately after the swap is transacted
D. no less than 24 hours after the completion of the swap

Correct Answer: C Section: Volume A

QUESTION 41
Which of the following statements is true?

A. Prices quoted by brokers should be taken to be firm in marketable amounts unless otherwise qualified
B. Prices quoted by brokers should be taken to be indicative in marketable amounts unless otherwise qualified
C. Prices quoted by brokers should be taken to be firm in amounts of 1,000,000.00 of the quoted currency unless otherwise qualified
D. Prices quoted by brokers should be taken to be indicative in amounts of 1,000,000.00 of the base currency unless otherwise qualified

Correct Answer: A Section: Volume A

QUESTION 42
A broker offers a dealer a financial incentive in the form of a price reduction to the previously agreed brokerage arrangements between the firms.

A. This is considered as a normal discount for bulk business.
B. The offer should be agreed only by directors or senior management on each side and should be recorded in writing.
C. The offer should be expressly approved by both the individuals concerned and clearly recorded in writing.
D. The Model Code strongly discourages such practices.

Correct Answer: B Section: Volume A

QUESTION 43
What ought to be done in the event a trade erroneously occurs at an off-market rate?

A. By agreement between the two counterparties, the trade must be cancelled as soon as practically possible since a rate amendment is prohibited.
B. By agreement between the two counterparts, the trade should, as soon as practically possible, either be cancelled or have its rate amended to an appropriate market rate.
C. The off-market rate should be adjusted as soon as possible to the appropriate current market rate and a new authenticated SWIFT confirmation sent immediately to the counterparty.
D. Nothing need be done, since once a trade is agreed to by the front office it is a binding agreement for both counterparties.

Correct Answer: B Section: Volume A

QUESTION 44
How long does the Model Code recommend that tapes and other records of dealers/brokers be kept?

A. at least two months
B. one year
C. up to one month
D. at least three months

Correct Answer: A Section: Volume A

QUESTION 45
What is the meaning of "under reference" in the terminology of trading?

A. a term the quoting dealer uses to caution the receiver of the quote that the price may have to be re-quoted at the receiver's risk
B. the qualification that the rate quoted in the market may no longer be valid and requires confirmation before any trades can be agreed upon
C. the statement that the rates quoted by the broker are for indication only
D. an acknowledgement by the dealer receiving the quote that the rate may have to be re-quoted at the receiver's risk

Correct Answer: B Section: Volume A

QUESTION 46
You request use of funds from your agent bank for 1 day on an amount of EUR 100,000,000.00, EONIA was 0.812% and the ECB deposit facility rate is 0.50%. What use of funds settlement amount should you expect?

A. EUR 1,388,89
B. EUR 1,561.11
C. EUR 2,255.56
D. EUR 2,951.39

Correct Answer: B Section: Volume A

QUESTION 47
If the value date of a forward USD/JPY transaction is declared a holiday in either New York or Tokyo, the correct value date will be:

A. the value date of the financial centre that is open
B. the next business day of the financial centre which is closed
C. the next business day when both New York and Tokyo are open
D. the previous business day when both New York and Tokyo are open

Correct Answer: C Section: Volume A

QUESTION 48
How frequently should business contingency procedures be tested and updated?

A. quarterly tests I updates as needed
B. at least every second year
C. half-yearly tests / yearly updates
D. at least yearly

Correct Answer: D Section: Volume A

QUESTION 49
Which of the following does the Model Code mention with regards to recording telephone conversations?

A. There is no need to inform new counterparties and clients that conversations will be recorded.
B. It is normal practice that tapes and other records should be kept for at least twelve months.

C. The periods for which tapes and other records should be retained should reflect the way in which the terms and conditions of transactions have been agreed, and the duration of transactions.
D. Dealers and other staff are reminded that telephones and electronic text messaging systems in the firm are intended for business and private use and that conversations and exchanges of text messages should be conducted in a casual manner.

Correct Answer: C Section: Volume A

QUESTION 50
Regarding access to production systems, which of the following is incorrect?

A. Profiles for functions are encouraged and should be reviewed semi-annually by a manager.
B. Developers should have unrestricted access to production systems.
C. Access to production systems should be rigorously controlled.
D. Users should not have access to change system functionalities.

Correct Answer: B Section: Volume A

QUESTION 51
Which one of the following statements is true?

A. Brokers should only show the names of banks to counterparties who have prime credit ratings.
B. Brokers should only show the names of banks to counterparties who provide good liquidity to the brokered market.
C. Brokers should only show the names of banks to counterparties whom they know well.
D. Brokers should only show the names of bank counterparties if both sides display a serious intention to transact

Correct Answer: D Section: Volume A

QUESTION 52
When do bank participants have a duty to make absolutely clear whether the prices they are quoting are firm or merely indicative?

A. only if they are dealing with brokers
B. only if dealing on an e-trading platform
C. only if they are dealing in non-marketable amounts
D. always

Correct Answer: D Section: Volume A

QUESTION 53
The use of standard settlement instructions (SSI's) is strongly encouraged because:

A. it reduces operational risk
B. it splits differences arising from failed settlement between the two counterparties
C. it removes the need for sending out SWIFT confirmations
D. the use of SSI's secures the trading on more secure platforms

Correct Answer: A Section: Volume A

QUESTION 54
Which of the following statements is true concerning dealing and rollovers at non-current rates?

A. When setting the rates for an FX swap to extend the maturity, the spot rate should be fixed immediately within the current spread
B. Where the use of non-current rates may be necessary, they should only be entered into with the prior explicit permission of the quoting party's senior management
C. Dealing and rollovers at non-current rates are relatively common market practice and therefore should not be treated differently from any other transaction
D. Dealing and rollovers at non-current rates are forbidden as they can help perpetrate fraud and tax evasion

Correct Answer: A Section: Volume A

QUESTION 55
A bank that has quoted a firm price is obliged to deal:

A. At that price
B. At that price in a marketable amount
C. At that price in a marketable amount, provided the counterparty's name is acceptable
D. At that price in a marketable amount, provided the counterparty's name is acceptable and the market price has not moved excessively

Correct Answer: C Section: Volume A

QUESTION 56

Confirmations of non-prime brokerage deals using CLS should be exchanged:

A. within 2 hours after deal agreed with counterparty
B. before the value date of the trade
C. by the end of the trade date
D. within 24 hours

Correct Answer: A Section: Volume A

QUESTION 57

Your agent bank accepts your back-valuation request for 1 day on an amount of EUR 50,000,000.00. EONIA is 0.375% and the ECB marginal lending facility rate is 1.50%. Applying conventional administration fees, how much will this be charged?

A. EUR 620.83
B. EUR 868.06
C. EUR 968.06
D. EUR 2,183.33

Correct Answer: C Section: Volume A

QUESTION 58

A 3-month (91-day) deposit of AUD 25,000,000.00 is made at 3.25%. At maturity, it is rolled over three times at 3.55% for 90 days, 4.15% for 91 days and 4.19% for 89 days. At the end of 12 months, how much is repaid (principal plus interest)?

A. AUD 25,962,011.00
B. AUD 25,959,714.91
C. AUD 25,948,878.47
D. AUD 25,948,648.82

Correct Answer: A Section: Volume A

QUESTION 59
Which of the following rates represents the highest investment yield in the Euromarket?

A. Semi-annual bond yield of 3.75%
B. Annual bond yield of 3.75%
C. Semi-annual money market yield of 3.75%
D. Annual money market rate of 3.75%s

Correct Answer: C Section: Volume A

QUESTION 60
It is June. You are over-borrowed from October to January on your deposit book. How would you hedge using FRAs?

A. Sell 3x6
B. Buy 3x6
C. Sell 4x7
D. Buy 4x7

Correct Answer: C Section: Volume B

QUESTION 61
Today, you sold 10 December EURODOLLAR futures contracts at 99.50. The closing price is fixed by the exchange at 99.375. What variation margin will be due?

A. You will have to pay USD 312.50
B. You will receive USD 312.50
C. You will have to pay USD 3,125.00
D. You will receive USD 3,125.00

Correct Answer: D Section: Volume B

QUESTION 62
What is a short straddle option strategy?

A. A long call option + long put option with the same strike prices
B. A short call option + short put option with the same strike prices
C. A long call option + short put option with the same strike prices
D. A short call option + long put option with the same strike prices

Correct Answer: B Section: Volume B

QUESTION 63
What is the probability of an 'at-the-money' option being exercised?

A. Less than 50% probability
B. 50% probability
C. More than 50% probability
D. Zero probability

Correct Answer: B Section: Volume B

QUESTION 64
What is a short strangle option strategy?

A. A short call option + long put option with a higher strike price than the call option
B. A long call option + long put option with a lower strike price than the call option
C. A short call option + short put option with a lower strike price than the call option
D. A long call option + long put option with higher strike price than the call option

Correct Answer: C Section: Volume B

QUESTION 65
A euro zone-based bank that is asset-sensitive to market interest rate changes might reduce interest rate risk by:

A. entering into a pay fixed I receive variable standard interest rate swap
B. entering into a receive fixed I pay variable standard interest rate swap
C. entering into a pay fixed / receive variable amortizing interest rate swap
D. entering into a GBP/USD FX swap

Correct Answer: B Section: Volume B

QUESTION 66
Which of the following statements about leverage ratios under Basel III is correct?

A. The leverage ratio is the ratio of the bank's Tier 1 Capital to total assets of the bank, excluding its off- balance sheet exposures and derivatives.
B. The purpose of introducing a leverage ratio is to avoid the build-up of excess leverage that could potentially lead to a "credit crunch" in stressed conditions.

C. The leverage ratio under Basel III must be higher than 4%.
D. The leverage ratio is the ratio of the bank's Tier 1 and Tier 2 Capital to total assets of the bank, including its off-balance sheet exposures and derivatives.

Correct Answer: B Section: Volume B

QUESTION 67
Complete the following sentence. If a bank has an asset repricing in 6 months funded by a liability repriced in 3 months:

A. the bank would benefit from higher interest rates
B. the bank could hedge this interest rate risk with a 3x6 derivative
C. the bank will make mark-to-market losses if rates decrease
D. the bank could hedge this interest rate risk by selling a 6x9 derivative

Correct Answer: A Section: Volume B

QUESTION 68
The Liquidity Coverage Ratio (LCR) in Basel III:

A. is a new rule that compares liquid asset levels in banks to their available equity capital
B. spells out a modernized system for calculating the required minimum reserve that banks must hold at the central bank
C. compares liquid and reliably liquidating assets to expected cash outflows from specified run-off rates for various liability classes under a short-term stress scenario
D. tied directly into the internal ratings-based approach for determining the liquidity of credit-counterparties

Correct Answer: B Section: Volume B

QUESTION 69
What is interest rate immunization in the context of bank gap management?

A. the strategy of holding more interest rate sensitive assets than interest rate sensitive liabilities
B. the strategy of holding fewer interest rate sensitive assets than interest rate sensitive liabilities
C. reducing the size of the balance sheet
D. structuring a bank's portfolio so that its net interest revenue and/or the market value of its portfolio will not be adversely affected by changes in interest rates

Correct Answer: C Section: Volume B

QUESTION 70
The weighted average duration of liabilities can be increased by:

A. buying additional 30-year German Government bonds
B. selling futures contracts on 30-year German Government bonds
C. buying futures contracts on 10-year German Government bonds
D. exercising an early repayment option on a long-term senior borrowing

Correct Answer: D Section: Volume B

QUESTION 71
Prudential regulation of banking book liquidity risk is dealt with by the Basel Committee (Basel II / Basel III) in the context of:

A. capital adequacy regulations in Pillar 1
B. market risk and Tier 3 capital elements
C. internal management procedures subject to supervisory review in Pillar 2
D. market discipline, disclosure and transparency in Pillar 3

Correct Answer: B Section: Volume B

QUESTION 72
VaR increases with:

A. lower correlation of underlying risk factors
B. a shorter time horizon
C. a lower confidence level
D. a higher confidence level

Correct Answer: C Section: Volume B

QUESTION 73
Under Basel Rules, the Basic Indicator Approach is a regulatory framework for:

A. liquidity risk
B. business risk
C. operational risk
D. funding risk

Correct Answer: B Section: Volume B

QUESTION 74
Under Basel rules, expected credit loss is a function of which of the following sets of parameters:

A. 1 minus recovery rate, probability of default and exposure at default
B. exposure at origination, exposure at default and loss given default
C. loss given default, 1 minus recovery rate and exposure at default
D. exposure at origination, recovery rates and probability of default

Correct Answer: B Section: Volume B

QUESTION 75
Under Basel rules the risk weight for claims on unrated sovereigns and their cennl banks in the standardized approach is:
A. 75%
B. 100%
C. 150%
D. 350%

Correct Answer: D Section: Volume B

QUESTION 76
Under Basel rules the meaning of CCF is:

A. Currency Conversion Factor
B. Credit Conversion Factor
C. Credit Contribution Factor
D. Credit Collateralization Factor

Correct Answer: B Section: Volume B

QUESTION 77
What is meant by "turn of the month"?

A. the last calendar day of the month
B. the last bank business day of the month
C. value last business day of the month against first business day of the next month
D. value first business day of the month against last business day of the same month

Correct Answer: C Section: Volume B

QUESTION 78
In order to give a price in EUR/USD, the broker must:

A. know whether the European Central Bank or the Federal Reserve is in the market before quoting
B. be sure that the quoting bank's prices are not shared with other brokers
C. get the price from a bank or a bid and an offer from different banks in order to make a two-way price, because the broker cannot make prices on his own
D. make sure that the quoting banks have sufficient credit lines

Correct Answer: C Section: Volume B

QUESTION 79
In interbank trading, if a dealer is calling "off" at the same time as the broker is hitting a price:

A. no transaction should be concluded and the broker should inform both counterparties accordingly
B. a transaction should be concluded and the broker should inform both counterparties accordingly
C. the dealer has the choice of either concluding the transaction or not
D. the broker decides whether the transaction should be concluded or not

Correct Answer: B Section: Volume B

QUESTION 80
A dealer has been invited by a broker to go to an exclusive club for the third time in a week. He should:

A. agree, since entertainment is a normal part of business
B. refer this to senior management
C. agree but insist on paying half the cost
D. agree, if the broker pays for the event but does not attend it

Correct Answer: B Section: Volume B

QUESTION 81
What does the Model Code recommend regarding "entertainment and gifts"?

A. Management should monitor the form, frequency and cost of entertainment and gifts dealers receive, have a clearly articulated policy towards the giving/receipt of gifts and ensure the policy is enforced.
B. As gifts and entertainment may be offered in the normal course of business, employees can offer inducements to conduct business and solicit them from the personnel of other institutions.
C. Although management should not monitor the form, frequency or cost of entertainment/gifts dealers receive, they may have a policy towards the giving/receipt of gifts and ensure the policy is enforced.
D. Gifts or entertainment should never be offered in the normal course of business, and employees must never offer any inducements to conduct business, nor solicit them from other institutions.

Correct Answer: C Section: Volume B

QUESTION 82
Which one of the following is a major objective of ACI-The Financial Markets Association?

A. to promote globalization and deregulation of the financial markets
B. to maintain the professional level of competence and to disseminate a high level of ethical and professional behavior
C. to act as the official international market regulator in the absence of government regulation
D. to become the sole global corporation of wholesale financial market professionals

Correct Answer: B Section: Volume B

QUESTION 83
Which of the following is required for institutions acting as prime brokers?

A. They must remain neutral and stay out of disputes between their customers.
B. They must rely on the execution venue to resolve disputes.
C. They must delegate the resolution of broken trades downstream to their clients.
D. They must take responsibility for the swift resolution of any disputes.

Correct Answer: D Section: Volume B

QUESTION 84
When a deal is done via a broker:

A. it need not be confirmed between the counterparties as the broker confirms it immediately with both counterparties
B. it should also be confirmed directly between the two counterparties
C. it is important to note that broker confirmations are bilateral confirmations between the principals of the trade
D. the dealer should obtain acknowledgement that the deal has been agreed to but may assume agreement to the trade in the absence of such acknowledgement

Correct Answer: B Section: Volume B

QUESTION 85
Bank XYZ calls you for a quote in EUR/USD for EUR 50,000,000.00. If you decide to quote, which of the following is true?

A. You must be prepared to deal EUR 50,000,000.00.
B. You may quote without stating the amount you are prepared to deal.
C. You are only committed to deal in a marketable amount.
D. You must be prepared to deal for more than EUR 50,000,000.00 in case Bank XYZ wishes to.

Correct Answer: A Section: Volume B

QUESTION 86
What happens if an instruction remains unmatched and/or unsettled through CLS Bank?

A. If there is more than one FX trade with a single counterparty to settle in the identical currencies, then both sides should bilaterally agree to settle the trades outside of CLS Bank on a net basis.
B. If there is only one FX trade with a single counterparty to settle in the identical currencies, then either side can unilaterally decide to settle the trade outside of CLS Bank on a net basis.
C. If there is more than one FX trade with a single counterparty to settle in the identical currencies, then both sides should bilaterally agree to settle the trade outside CLS Bank on a gross basis.
D. If there is more than one FX trade with a single counterparty to settle in the identical currencies, then either side can unilaterally instruct the CLS Bank to settle the trades.

Correct Answer: C Section: Volume B

QUESTION 87
What recommendation does the Model Code make to banks accepting a stop-loss order?

A. The Model Code emphasizes the importance of clear, concise documentation and on-going lines of communication.
B. Bank management must guarantee a fixed price execution to the counterparty.
C. The Model Code recommends that only experienced dealers should be allowed to take such orders.
D. Bank staff must secure the approval of the counterparty's management to accept such orders.

Correct Answer: A Section: Volume B

QUESTION 88
Where sale and repurchase agreements or stock borrowing or lending transactions are entered into:

A. screen services, brokers and other third party providers can all be useful sources of data
B. For periods less than one month, the maturity date will be the first date that is a business day that is within one, seven, fourteen days from the value date, but when near the month end must never be a date in the next calendar month
C. Inter-dealer brokers or the automated trading system need not be notified when participants attempt to utilize odd settlement dates
D. It is not recommended that legal opinion should be obtained on the enforceability of the contract

Correct Answer: A Section: Volume B

QUESTION 89
Whose compliance rules, regulations and best practices should be followed in FX electronic trading?

A. solely those of the electronic trading platforms vendors
B. exclusively ACI's Model Code Best Practices
C. ACI's Model Code Best Practices and ICMA's Market Practice & Regulatory Policy
D. the electronic trading platforms vendors' and the ACIs Model Code Best Practices guidelines

Correct Answer: B Section: Volume B

QUESTION 90
You quote a price to a broker. It is hit by another bank, but you are not informed until some time afterward that the deal has been done. Who is to blame?
A. You are, as it is your responsibility to check periodically that the price has not been dealt upon.
B. The broker is, as he must immediately tell you that your price has been dealt upon.
C. The other bank is, since it did not immediately seek confirmation.
D. All the parties, particularly you and the other bank.

Correct Answer: B Section: Volume B

QUESTION 91
For which of the following might an MT370 be used?

A. To confirm an FX transaction
B. To advise the netting position of a currency in NDFS
C. To advise changes in SSIs
D. To confirm a MM transaction

Correct Answer: B Section: Volume B

QUESTION 92
What steps will the CFP of the ACI probably not undertake after having been formally notified by one of the parties of a breach of the letter or spirit of the Model Code?

A. consult the local ACI national association
B. bring the matter to the appropriate court of justice
C. examine the complaint
D. bring the matter to the attention of the appropriate regulatory body

Correct Answer: B Section: Volume B

QUESTION 93
Experience has shown that recourse to taped telephone conversations proves invaluable to the speedy resolution of disputes. Therefore, the Model Code recommends:

A. that all telephone conversations (internal and external) be taped without informing counterparties
B. that only conversations undertaken by dealers and brokers should be recorded

C. that all conversations undertaken by dealers and brokers should be recorded, together with back office telephone lines used by those responsible for confirming deals or passing payments to other institutions
D. that only telephone conversations between dealers and brokers be recorded

Correct Answer: D Section: Volume B

QUESTION 94
Which of the following correctly states the Model Code's recommendations regarding electronic trading and broking?

A. Liquidity providers should be cognizant of reputational risks when supplying liquidity for onward third party consumption.
B. Market participants must not seek information as to the legal status of a potential counterparty before allocating credit or trading status.
C. Transactions should be handled in accordance with the regulator's dealing rule book.
D. Access to systems internally and at the client interface must be strictly controlled by the dealers.

Correct Answer: A Section: Volume B

QUESTION 95
A US security yields 7% on an annually-compounded bond basis. What is the equivalent annually- compounded money market yield?

A. 7.09%
B. 7.03%
C. 6.90%
D. 6.95%

Correct Answer: C Section: Volume B

QUESTION 96
Today's spot value date is the 29th of February. What is the maturity date of a 4-month USD deposit deal today? Assume no bank holidays.

A. Thursday 27th June
B. Friday 28th June
C. Saturday 29th June
D. Monday 1st July

Correct Answer: B Section: Volume B

QUESTION 97
From the following AUD rates:

3M AUD (91-day) deposits   2.35%   3x6 AUD (90-day) FRA   2.55%

Calculate the 6-month implied cash rate.
A. 2.37%
B. 2.46%
C. 2.55%
D. 4.90%

Correct Answer: B
Section: Volume B

QUESTION 98
Which is the day count/annual basis convention for SGD money market deposits?

A. ACT/365
B. ACT/360
C. ACT/ACT
D. 30E/360

Correct Answer: A Section: Volume B

QUESTION 99
A 6-month (182-day) investment of CAD 15,500,000.00 yields a return of CAD 100,000.00. What is the rate of return?

A. 1.32%
B. 1.29%
C. 1.28%
D. 0.65%

Correct Answer: C Section: Volume B

QUESTION 100
Which of the following are specifically quoted in terms of a yield-to-maturity?

A. US Treasury bill
B. CD
C. Interbank deposit
D. USCP

Correct Answer: B Section: Volume B

QUESTION 101
Who takes the counterparty risk on the seller in a to-party repo?

A. The buyer
B. The to-party agent
C. A third-party guarantor
D. A central clearing counterparty

Correct Answer: A Section: Volume B

QUESTION 102
Repo is said to have "double indemnity" due to the creditworthiness of the counterparty and:

A. A written legal agreement between the parties
B. The oversight of the transaction by the custodian of the collateral
C. The creditworthiness of the collateral
D. The right of close-out and set-off in an event of default

Correct Answer: C Section: Volume B

QUESTION 103
In which type of repo is "double dipping" a risk?

A. Delivery repo
B. HIC repo
C. To-party repo
D. "Double dipping" is never a risk in any type of repo

Correct Answer: B Section: Volume B

QUESTION 104
You buy a 30-day 4% CD with a face value of GBP 20,000,000.00 at par when it is issued. You sell it in the secondary market after 10 days at 4.05%. What is your holding period yield?

A. 4.05%
B. 3.891%
C. 3.838%
D. 1.946%

Correct Answer: B Section: Volume B

QUESTION 105
What are the secondary market proceeds of a CD with a face value of EUR 5,000,000.00 and a coupon of 3% that was issued at par for 182 days and is now trading at 3% but with only 7 days remaining to maturity?

A. EUR 4,997,085.03
B. EUR 5,000,000.00
C. EUR 5,071,086.45
D. EUR 5,072,874.16

Correct Answer: D Section: Volume B

QUESTION 106
The spot/next repo rate for the 5% Bund 2018 is quoted to you at 1.75- 80%. You sell bonds with a market value of EUR 5,798,692.00 through a sell/buy-back. The Repurchase Price is:

A. EUR 5,798,982
B. EUR 5,799,497
C. EUR 5,746,376
D. EUR 5,000,694

Correct Answer: A Section: Volume B

QUESTION 107
The one-month (31-day) GC repo rate for French government bonds is quoted to you at 3.75- 80%. As collateral, you are offered EUR 25,000,000.00 nominal of the 5.5% OAT April 2012, which is worth EUR 28,137,500.00.

The Repurchase Price is:

A. EUR 28,228,360.69
B. EUR 28,229,572.15
C. EUR 25,080,729.18
D. EUR 25,081,805.55

Correct Answer: A Section: Volume B

QUESTION 108
If 6-month USD/CAD forward rates are quoted at 40/45, which of the following statements is correct?

A. USD rates are higher than CAD rates in the 6-month
B. CAD rates are higher than USD rates in the 6-month

C. There is a positive USD yield curve
D. There is not enough information to decide

Correct Answer: B **Section: Volume B**

QUESTION 109
What is the ISO code for the currency of China?

A. CHY
B. CNR
C. CHR
D. CNY

Correct Answer: D

Section: Volume B

QUESTION 110
The "spot basis" of a 2 against 4 months EUR/USD forward/forward swap is:

A. usually the current spot EUR/USD mid-market rate
B. commonly the prevailing 4-month forward EUR/USD mid-rate
C. always the forward EUR/USD bid rate of the first swap leg
D. generally the prevailing 2-month forward EUR/USD mid-rate

Correct Answer: D **Section: Volume B**

QUESTION 111
If you sell USD 3-month forward to a client against EUR, what should you do to hedge your position?

A. Buy a 3-month EUR/USD outright forward
B. Buy USD spot, and sell and buy a 3-month EUR/USD FX swap
C. Sell EUR/USD in the spot market, lend EUR for 3 months and borrow USD for 3 months
D. Sell EUR/USD in the spot market, borrow EUR for 3 months and lend USD for 3 months

Correct Answer: D **Section: Volume B**

QUESTION 112
What is an FX swap from spot?

A. An exchange of two streams of interest payments in different currencies and an exchange of the principal amounts of those currencies at maturity
B. A spot sale (purchase) and a forward purchase (sale) of two currencies agreed simultaneously between two parties
C. An exchange of currencies on a date beyond spot and at a price fixed today
D. An agreement to buy (sell) an amount of base currency value spot and simultaneously resell (buy back) the same amount to the same counterpart value today

Correct Answer: B Section: Volume B

QUESTION 113
Which of the following currency risks could only be hedged by a non deliverable forward (NDF)?

A. an exposure in Latvian Lats (LVL)
B. an exposure in Russian Rouble (RUB)
C. an exposure in Romanian Leu (RON)
D. an exposure in Bulgarian Lev (BGN)

Correct Answer: B Section: Volume B

QUESTION 114
A 6-month SEK/NOK Swap is quoted 40/50. Spot is 1.1145. Which of the following statements is correct?

A. SEK interest rates are higher than NOK interest rates
B. NOK interest rates are higher than SEK interest rates
C. NOK interest rates are higher than USD interest rates
D. SEK interest rates and NOK interest rates are converging

Correct Answer: B Section: Volume B

QUESTION 115
For which country's currency is ZAR the ISO code?

A. Saudi Arabia
B. South Africa
C. Zimbabwe
D. Zambia
Correct Answer: B Section: Volume B

QUESTION 116
You are quoted the following rates:

Spot GBP/USD   1.5295-00
Spot USD/CHF   0.9320-23
6M GBP/USD swap   16/12
6M USD/CHF swap   22/18

Where can you buy GBP against CHF 6-month outright? A. 1.4206
B. 1.4215
C. 1.4217
D. 1.4225
Correct Answer: D Section: Volume B

QUESTION 117
You are quoted spot USD/NOK 5.7220-28 and USD/SEK 6.3850-58, at what price can you buy NOK against SEK?

A. 0.8963
B. 1.1157
C. 1.1159
D. 1.1160
Correct Answer: D Section: Volume B

QUESTION 118
You are quoted the following market rates:

Spot EUR/USD 1.3150 3M (92-day) EUR 0.20%
3M (92-day) USD 0.44%
What is 3-month EUR/USD?

A. 1.3159
B. 1.3158
C. 1.3142
D. 1.3230
Correct Answer: B Section: Volume B

QUESTION 119
You are quoted the following market rates:

Spot AUD/CAD 1.0600 12M (360-day) AUD 3.40%
12M (360-day) CAD 1.55%

What are the 12-month AUD/CAD forward points? A. +190
B. -193
C. -192
D. -190

Correct Answer: D Section: Volume B

QUESTION 120
You are quoted the following rates:

Spot GBP/CHF 1.4535-45
3M GBP/CHF swap 22/19

At what rate can you sell GBP against CHF outright 3-month? A. 1.4523
B. 1.4526
C. 1.4513
D. 1.4516

Correct Answer: C Section: Volume B

QUESTION 121
An interest rate swap (IRS) is:

A. A contract to exchange one stream of interest payments for another
B. A temporary exchange of one deposit for another of a longer maturity in the same currency
C. A forward-forward contract
D. A contract to exchange an interest rate stream in one currency for another one in a different currency

Correct Answer: A Section: Volume B

QUESTION 122
An important reason for trading a futures contract rather than an FRA is:

A. The expense of settling an FRA
B. The reduced counterparty risk on a futures exchange
C. The reduced basis risk on futures
D. The superior interest rate risk on FRAs

Correct Answer: B Section: Volume B

QUESTION 123
Selling a FRA has the same interest rate exposure as:

A. Opening a positive gap
B. Going over-borrowed
C. Making a forward-forward loan
D. Taking a forward-forward deposit

Correct Answer: C Section: Volume B

QUESTION 124
What is the purpose of an initial margin on a futures exchange?

A. To cover losses incurred between variation margin payments
B. To exclude retail investors
C. To pay reserve requirements
D. To cover fees due to the clearing house

Correct Answer: A Section: Volume B

QUESTION 125
What is the Overnight Index for USD?

A. H-15 Index
B. Prime Rate
C. Overnight Fed funds
D. Fed funds effective rate

Correct Answer: D Section: Volume B

QUESTION 126
Which of the following statements is correct?

A. An adjusted settlement amount is paid at the end of the FRA contract period that includes reinvestment interest for late payment
B. An unadjusted settlement amount is paid at the end of the FRA contract period
C. An adjusted settlement amount is paid at the start of the FRA contract period that is discounted for early payment
D. An unadjusted settlement amount is paid at the start of the FRA contract period

Correct Answer: C Section: Volume B

QUESTION 127
A forward-forward lender has an exposure to the risk of:

A. Higher interest rates
B. Lower interest rates
C. Flattening yield curve
D. Parallel shift downwards in the yield curve

Correct Answer: A Section: Volume B

QUESTION 128
What is the Overnight Index for GBP?

A. SONIA
B. STINA
C. STONIA
D. EONIA

Correct Answer: A Section: Volume B

QUESTION 129
Claims should be communicated in writing via e-mail or preferably by authenticated SWIFT. What information should be provided in the claim?

A. the details of the transaction involved, the number of days the payment was delayed and the resulting cost
B. the details of the transaction involved, the number of days the payment was delayed and the cost, together with Central Bank rate to be applied
C. the details of the transaction involved, the number of days the payment

was delayed and the cost, together with reference rates to be applied
D. the details of the transaction involved, the number of days the payment was delayed and the cost, together with the calculation methodology being claimed

Correct Answer: D Section: Volume C

QUESTION 130
You and a dealer at another bank have a verbal bilateral reciprocal arrangement to quote each other two-way prices. During periods of high volatility, the other dealer refuses to quote to you. What does the Model Code say about this situation?

A. The other dealer is bound to reciprocate.
B. This is not in any way an enforceable or binding commitment.
C. The Model Code does not comment on dealing reciprocity.
D. It is common market practice to suspend reciprocity in periods of high volatility.

Correct Answer: B Section: Volume C

QUESTION 131
What does the Model Code say about omitting the "big figure" in voice communication?

A. The "big figure" should not be included in outright quotations.
B. In order to avoid misunderstandings, the "big figure" should not be mentioned when repeating the details (facts/rates) of the deal.
C. For the sake of brevity and efficiency, "big figures" should never be quoted at all in spot FX trading.
D. The Model Code recommends that the "big figure" be included in all outright and spot FX quotations.

Correct Answer: D Section: Volume C

QUESTION 132
Which of the following risks is best mitigated by CLS?

A. currency risk
B. operational risk
C. liquidity risk
D. settlement risk

Correct Answer: D Section: Volume C

QUESTION 133
When differences in payment arise because of errors in the payment of funds:

A. claims should be made for the costs incurred by the injured party and include all administration costs
B. no party involved can be enforced to contribute to achieve an equitable resolution to the problem
C. no market participant should be unjustly enriched or injured by the action/error of another market participant
D. claims are calculated on the full principal amount of the failed payment with the interest rate imposed by the injured party

Correct Answer: C Section: Volume C

QUESTION 134
The Model Code stipulates that you have a right to qualify your quotes in terms of amounts:

A. if you do so when you make the price
B. provided the amounts are marketable
C. once you have discovered the name of the counterparty for credit reasons
D. at anytime

Correct Answer: A Section: Volume C

QUESTION 135
As regards controls, which of the following best practices for counterparty identification is incorrect?

A. Amendments to customer standing data should be subject to 4 eyes control and only changed if the appropriately authorized documentation is provided.
B. The set up of settlement instructions and the confirmation method should be fixed when setting the first transaction.
C. No trading should be done without first identifying and setting up the counterparty.
D. Counterparty identification and setup of settlement instructions should be completed in less than 2 working days.

Correct Answer: B Section: Volume C

QUESTION 136
What does the Model Code say concerning repos and stock-lending?

A. Legal documentation must be put in place as soon as possible after transaction.
B. All market participants should use the Modified Previous Business Day Convention.
C. The exact maturity (end) dates for transactions must be agreed as soon as possible after a transaction.
D. All market participants should use the Modified Following Business Day Convention.

Correct Answer: D Section: Volume C

QUESTION 137
What should be done when a voice broker hits a dealer's price as "done" at the very instant the dealer calls "off"?

A. The deal should not be concluded and the broker should inform both counterparties accordingly.
B. The transaction should be concluded and the broker should inform both counterparties accordingly.
C. The broker should immediately inform both counterparties that the deal will have to be renegotiated.
D. The broker should decide whether the transaction is concluded or not and inform both counterparties accordingly.

Correct Answer: B Section: Volume C

QUESTION 138
Which of the following does the Model Code not recommend to prevent technical errors by etrading devices?

A. A manual "kill button" to disable the system's ability to trade and cancel all resting orders.
B. An 'inbound message rate" feature that monitors the number of confirmation messages that are sent from trading venues within a specific time period.
C. A "repeated automated execution throttle" monitoring the frequency of strategies that are filled and then re-entered into the market without human intervention through automated trading systems.
D. A "fat-finger quantity" feature limiting the size of orders that can be sent from the trading systems and preventing order quantities above the fat-finger limit from leaving the system.

Correct Answer: B Section: Volume C

QUESTION 139
In trade confirmation, which one of the following statements about "matching" is correct?

A. matching should be performed by no later than the day after trading day
B. matching processes are manual and may not be automated
C. matching should be performed as soon as possible upon receipt of the confirmation
D. confirmation matching should be a post-settlement workflow activity

Correct Answer: C Section: Volume C

QUESTION 140
If several banks hit a broker simultaneously for an amount greater than the amount for which the price was shown:

A. no transaction is done
B. the broker has to honor each and every amount hit
C. the broker has to split the amount among the banks on a pro rata basis
D. the broker may freely choose the bank(s) he will deal with

Correct Answer: C Section: Volume C

QUESTION 141
According the Model Code, a principal, whose name has been rejected, feeling that the broker may have actually quoted a price or rate that it could not in fact substantiate, may:

A. deduct points from the broker or adjust the brokerage bill accordingly
B. in some centres, ask either the central bank or some other neutral body to investigate and confidentially verify that there was support for the original price or rate
C. in some centres, ask the local ACI to investigate and confidentially verify that there was support for the original price or rate
D. insist that the broker discloses the name of the other counterparty

Correct Answer: B Section: Volume C

QUESTION 142
What kind of information should dealers and brokers take care when relaying?

A. Information that could be damaging to a third party
B. Unsubstantiated rumours
C. Unsubstantiated information that they suspect may be inaccurate and damaging to a third party
D. Price-sensitive information

Correct Answer: C Section: Volume C

QUESTION 143
Which of the following is true regarding the consummation of a deal?

A. verbal agreements are considered binding
B. written confirmations always override terms verbally agreed to
C. deals agreed to verbally can be done subject to documentation
D. verbal agreements are never to be considered legally binding

Correct Answer: C Section: Volume C

QUESTION 144
Which of the following dealing strategies involves the placing of orders with very short quote lives into a market?

A. frequency trading
B. high-incidence trading
C. flash trading
D. liquidity aggregators

Correct Answer: C Section: Volume C

QUESTION 145
A 3-month (90-day) NZD deposit is 2.75% and 6-month (180-day) NZD deposit is 3.00%. What is the 3x6 NZD deposit rate?

A. 3.2281%
B. 3.2278%
C. 3.00%
D. 2.875%

Correct Answer: B Section: Volume C

QUESTION 146
What is the name of the reference against which most USD and JPY deposits and loans are fixed in London?

A. EURIBOR
B. EONIA
C. LIBOR
D. SONIA

Correct Answer: C Section: Volume C

QUESTION 147
You borrow GBP 2,500,000.00 at 0.625% for 165 days. How much do you repay including interest?

A. GBP 2,507,161.46
B. GBP 2,507,063.36
C. GBP 2,507,006.85
D. GBP 2,507,106.16

Correct Answer: B Section: Volume C

QUESTION 148
The columns below list short-term cash rates on 3rd April and 3rd F1ay
3rd April 3rd May

	3rd April	3rd May
T/N	5.55%	3.99%
S/N	5.41%	3.99%
1W	5.27%	4.01%
2W	5.17%	4.02%
1M	4.95%	4.05%
2M	4.81%	4.07%
3M	4.69%	4.09%
6M	4.51%	4.14%
12M	4.25%	4.25%

Describe the shape of the short-term segment of the yield curve on 3' April using market terminology. In addition, describe the change in the shape of the curve between 3rd April and 3rd May.

A. Positive, steepening
B. Positive, flattening
C. Inverted, steepening
D. Inverted, flattening

Correct Answer: C Section: Volume C

QUESTION 149
7-day USCP is quoted at a rate of discount of 1.75%. What is its true yield?

A. 1.73%
B. 1.75%
C. 1.77%
D. 1.80%

Correct Answer: B Section: Volume C

QUESTION 150
You have quoted your customer the following CAD deposit rates:

1M 1.00-05%
2M 1.06-11%
3M 1.13-18%

The customer says, "I give you CAD 20,000,000.00 in the two's". What have you done?

A. Borrowed CAD 20,000,000.00 at 1.06%
B. Lent CAD 20,000,000.00 at 1.11%
C. Borrowed CAD 20,000,000.00 at 1.11%
D. Lent CAD 20,000,000.00 at 1.06%
Correct Answer: A Section: Volume C

QUESTION 151
Which of the following may pay a return as a mix of income and capital/gain loss?

A. CD
B. Interbank deposit
C. Classic repo
D. Treasury bill
Correct Answer: A Section: Volume C

QUESTION 152
Which of the following is not transferable?

A. Euro certificate of deposit
B. US Treasury bill
C. CP
D. Call deposit

Correct Answer: D Section: Volume C

QUESTION 153
What happens when the issuer of a bond being used as collateral in a classic repo fails to pay a coupon on the bond during the term of the repo?

A. The transaction is terminated and the collateral is returned to the seller
B. The transaction is rolled over until the coupon is paid or the issuer becomes insolvent, at which point the seller becomes an unsecured creditor of the issuer
C. The buyer is obliged to make a manufactured payment to the seller and becomes an unsecured creditor of the issuer
D. The buyer is not obliged to make a manufactured payment to the seller but the buyer is likely to ask for margin

Correct Answer: D Section: Volume C

QUESTION 154
What is the Repurchase Price of a classic repo?

A. The market value of bond collateral at the end of the repo at the clean price of the bond
B. The market value of bond collateral at the end of the repo at the dirty price of the bond
C. The amount of cash actually paid for collateral at the start of the repo
D. The amount of cash actually paid for collateral at the start of the repo plus repo interest

Correct Answer: D Section: Volume C

QUESTION 155
A CD with a face value of USD 50,000,000.00 and a coupon of 4.50% was issued at par for 90 days and is now trading at 4.50% with 30 days remaining to maturity. What has been the capital gain or loss since issue?

A. +USD 373,599.00
B. +USD 186,099.00
C. -USD 1,400.99
D. Nil

Correct Answer: C Section: Volume C

QUESTION 156
You buy a 181-day 2.75% CD with a face value of USD 1,500,000.00 at par when it is issued. You sell it in the secondary market after 150 days at 2.60%. What is your holding period yield?

A. 2.60%
B. 2.75%
C. 2.775%
D. 2.813%

Correct Answer: C Section: Volume C

QUESTION 157
The Interest Rate Parity Theorem should work because, when one sells a low interest rate currency to invest in a high interest rate currency and hedges the currency risk:

A. The cost of hedging is given by the forward points, which are equal to the interest rate differential between the two currencies
B. The high interest rate currency will depreciate
C. The profit from the appreciation of the high interest rate currency has been hedged away
D. Interest rates are mean reverting, which means the low interest rate will tend to rise and the high interest rate will tend to fall

Correct Answer: A Section: Volume C

QUESTION 158
Which one of the following bullion coins has a 999.9/1000 gold purity (.9999 fineness)?

A. the Canadian "Maple Leaf"
B. the South African "Krugerand"
C. the American "Gold Eagle"
D. the United Kingdom "Sovereign"

Correct Answer: A Section: Volume C

QUESTION 159
What is the Gold Offered Forward Rate (GOFO)?

A. the price differential between spot and forward gold prices
B. the rate at which dealers will lend gold against US dollars
C. the implied forward price of gold
D. the price of gold for forward delivery

Correct Answer: B Section: Volume C

QUESTION 160
For which country's currency is SEK the ISO code?

A. South Korea
B. Sri Lanka
C. Slovakia
D. Sweden

Correct Answer: D Section: Volume C

QUESTION 161
3-month USD/CHF is quoted at 12/10. Interest rates in Switzerland are reduced but USD rates (which are higher) are unchanged. What would you expect the 3- month forward USD/CHF rate to be?

A. unchanged
B. 15/13
C. 10/8
D. 6/4

Correct Answer: B Section: Volume C

QUESTION 162
What is the ISO code for the Indian rupee?

A. IDR
B. RUP
C. INR
D. IND

Correct Answer: C **Section: Volume C**

QUESTION 163
Cable is quoted at 1.5575-80 and you say "5 yours!" to the broker. What have you done?

A. Sold USD 5,000,000.00 at 1.5575
B. Sold GBP 5,000,000.00 at 1.5575
C. Bought GBP 5,000,000.00 at 1.5580
D. Bought USD 5,000,000.00 at 1.5580

Correct Answer: B **Section: Volume C**

QUESTION 164
What is the result of combining a 1-month buy and sell FX swap with a 2-month sell and buy FX swap?

A. a 1x2 FRA short position
B. a 1- against 2-month buy and sell forward/forward FX swap
C. a 1- against 2-month sell and buy forward/forward FX swap
D. a 1- against 2-month forward/forward long position

Correct Answer: C **Section: Volume C**

QUESTION 165
USD/CHF is quoted to you at 0.9290-93 and GBP/USD at 1.5320-30. At what rate could you buy GBP and sell CHF?

A. 1.4242
B. 1.4232
C. 1.4246
D. 1.4237

Correct Answer: C **Section: Volume C**

QUESTION 166
Your GBP/CHF rate is 1.3710-15. How many GBP would your customer have to give you to buy CHF 10,000,000.00?

A. 7,291,286.91
B. 7,293,946.02
C. 13,710,000.00
D. 13,715,000.00

Correct Answer: B Section: Volume C

QUESTION 167
Using the following rates:

Spot GBP/CHF   1.4235-55
Spot CHF/SEK   6.8815-45 3M GBP/SEK swap   140/150

What is the price for 3-month outright GBP/SEK?

A. 9.8141-9.8246
B. 9.8108-9.8279
C. 9.8098-9.8289
D. 9.8151-9.8236

Correct Answer: A Section: Volume C

QUESTION 168
If GBP/USD is quoted to you at 1.6120-30, how much GBP would you receive if you sold USD 2,000,000.00?

A. 1,239,925.60
B. 1,237,873.80
C. 1,240,694.79
D. 1,242,720.50

Correct Answer: A Section: Volume C

QUESTION 169
Today is Monday, 8th December. You sell a 9x12 USD FRA for value Thursday, 10th September next year. On what date is the settlement amount due to be paid or received (assuming that there are no holidays)?

A. 8th September next year
B. 10th September next year
C. 8thDecembernextyear
D. December next year

Correct Answer: B Section: Volume C

QUESTION 170
An FRA is:

A. A cash instrument
B. An exchange traded derivative
C. An interest rate derivative
D. A balance sheet instrument

Correct Answer: C Section: Volume C

QUESTION 171
You are paying 1,00% per annum paid semi-annually and receiving 6-month LIBOR on a USD 10,000,000.00 interest rate swap with exactly two years to maturity. 6-month LIBOR for the next payment date is fixed today at 0.95%. How would you hedge the swap using FRAs?

How to hedge an IRS with a strip of FRAs?

A. buy a strip of 0x6, 6x12, 12x18 and 18x24 FRAs
B. sell a strip of 0x6, 6x12, 12x18 and 18x24 FRAs
C. buy a strip of 6x12, 12x18 and 18x24 FRAs
D. sell a strip of 6x12, 12x18 and 18x24 FRAs

Correct Answer: D Section: Volume C

QUESTION 172
How would you delta hedge a deeply "in-the-money" short put option?

A. Go short of the underlying commodity equal to 50% of the size of the option contract
B. Go long of the underlying commodity equal to 50% of the size of the option contract

C. Go long of the underlying commodity equal to more than 50% of the full size of the option contract
D. Go short of the underlying commodity equal to more than 50% of the full size of the option contract

Correct Answer: D Section: Volume C

QUESTION 173
An interest rate guarantee (IRG) is:

A. An FRA
B. An option on an FRA
C. A collar
D. An IRS

Correct Answer: B Section: Volume C

QUESTION 174
Which of the following statements is correct?

A. With liquidity transfer pricing (LTP) banks attribute the costs, benefits and risks of liquidity to respective business units within a bank
B. With liquidity transfer pricing (LTP) banks are monitoring and diversifying their funding base
C. With liquidity transfer pricing (LTP) banks are agreeing with external liquidity providers on the fair market price of funds
D. Liquidity transfer pricing charges providers of funds for the cost of liquidity and users of funds for the benefit of liquidity

Correct Answer: A Section: Volume C

QUESTION 175
The Liquidity Coverage Ratio imposed by Basel III requires a bank:

A. to keep enough highly liquid assets to cover its net liabilities for the next 10 days to guard against severe liquidity stress
B. to keep enough highly liquid assets to cover its net liabilities for the next 30 days to guard against severe liquidity stress
C. to keep enough highly liquid assets to cover its net liabilities for the next 60 days to guard against severe liquidity stress
D. to retain enough liquidity to cover its assets against severe default risk

Correct Answer: B Section: Volume C

QUESTION 176
Does the slope of the interest yield curve typically have a substantial impact on a bank's net interest margin?

A. No, it doesn't, since the slope of the yield cure is unrelated to the spread between short-term and long-term interest rates.
B. No, it doesn't. There isn't any link at all between the slope of the interest yield curve and a bank's net interest margin.
C. Yes it does. In banking, long-term rates usually apply to bank deposits and money market borrowings whereas short-term interest rates are attached to loans and securities.
D. Yes it does. Long-term rates usually apply to a bank's assets (loans, securities, etc.) and the short term interest rates are generally attached to liabilities (deposits, money market borrowings, etc.).

Correct Answer: D Section: Volume C

QUESTION 177
A purchased 3X6 FRA should be reported in a gap report as

A. a given deposit with a term of six months
B. a taken deposit with a term of three months
C. a given deposit with a term of three months and a taken deposit with a term of six months
D. a taken deposit with a term of three months and a given deposit with a term of six months

Correct Answer: C Section: Volume C

QUESTION 178
What would be the strategy for a bank if it is unable to speculate on interest rates and/or unable to absorb market risk?

A. to run a zero gap
B. to hold more interest rate sensitive assets than interest rate sensitive liabilities
C. to reduce the size of the balance sheet
D. to hold fewer interest rate sensitive assets than interest rate sensitive liabilities

Correct Answer: A Section: Volume C

QUESTION 179
Net funding requirements in liquidity management are determined by means of:

A. adding up expected vault cash outflows, ATMs and other cash points operated by the institution across all branches
B. establishing a forward cash flow plan that takes account of all contractual and behavioral cash flows related to assets and liabilities
C. the net cash flow from investment activities in the IFRS consolidated Statement of Cash Flows for prior periods
D. subtracting short-term liabilities from short-term assets

Correct Answer: B Section: Volume C

QUESTION 180
Which one of the following statements is incorrect under Basel III?

A. Instruments qualifying for recognition as Tier 1 or Tier 2 capital will be substantially restricted.
B. Basel III does not include Tier 3 capital
C. There is a distinction between upper Tier 2 and lower Tier 2 capital
D. New non-common equity Tier 1 and Tier 2 instruments are more loss-absorbing than previously

Correct Answer: C Section: Volume C

QUESTION 181
Which one of the following statements regarding the variance-covariance method for calculating value-at-risk is true?

A. The volatilities of the underlying assets are normally distributed and the prices remain constant.
B. The risk factors are normally distributed and volatilities of risk factors and correlations between risk factors are constant.
C. The prices of underlying assets are normally distributed, the volatilities of risk factors follow a GARCH process and correlations between risk factors are constant.
D. The returns of underlying assets are normally distributed and volatilities of risk factors and correlations between risk factors are constant.

Correct Answer: D Section: Volume C

QUESTION 182
Which one of the following formulae is correct?

A. Long a straight bond + pay fixed on a swap = long a synthetic Floating Rate Note
B. Long a straight bond + pay floating on a swap = long a synthetic Floating Rate Note
C. Short a straight bond + receive fixed on a swap = long a synthetic Floating Rate Note
D. Short a straight bond + pay fixed on a swap = long a synthetic Floating Rate Note

Correct Answer: A Section: Volume C

QUESTION 183
Under new Basel rules, what is the meaning of CVA?

A. Credit Value Adaption
B. Call Value Adaption
C. Credit Value Adjustment
D. Counterpart Value Adjustment

Correct Answer: C Section: Volume C

QUESTION 184
Which of the following does not represent an operational risk as defined by Basel rules?

A. theft of information
B. damage to an organization through loss of its reputation or standing
C. market manipulation
D. loss incurred from the use of incorrect documentation

Correct Answer: B Section: Volume C

QUESTION 185
You are a sales person in a bank and are about to sell a structured note to a non-professional customer. Before finalizing the transaction you remember to double- check the customer's charter. You learn that the customer is not allowed to invest in structured products. The risk you have avoided is most likely to be classified as:

A. credit risk
B. liquidity risk
C. legal risk
D. refinancing risk

Correct Answer: C Section: Volume C

QUESTION 186
By what means should a financial institution preferably submit SSI changes and notifications to its clients?

A. e-mail
B. fax or letter
C. MTn99 SWIFT message
D. MT670/671 SWIFT message

Correct Answer: D Section: Volume C

QUESTION 187
The Model Code's correct recommendation regarding electronic trading states:

A. Time stamps on e-trading platforms need to be internally and globally synchronised to ensure appropriate tracking of trades
B. All records should be archived and appropriate audit trails must be maintained as required by the local Central Bank
C. Regular tests for loss of access to external liquidity platforms but not loss of service to clients should be undertaken
D. Testing of the system's capability to cope with extreme volumes should be carried out annually

Correct Answer: A Section: Volume C

QUESTION 188
When can a broker consider a deal to be done?

A. if he is confident that the dealer will not back out of the deal
B. if both parties to the deal have established credit lines for each other
C. if one party to the deal acknowledges interest
D. if he receives acknowledgement from both the dealers involved

Correct Answer: D Section: Volume C

QUESTION 189
A dealer in the spot foreign exchange market has to assume that a price given to a voice broker is only valid:

A. for a short length of time, usually 30 seconds
B. until the price has been taken "off" by the dealer
C. for a short length of time, typically a matter of seconds
D. for a minute or two

Correct Answer: C Section: Volume C

QUESTION 190
As to the Charter of ACI - The Financial Markets Association, what do members not pledge?

A. to maintain the professional level of competence and the ethical standards of loyalty
B. to develop sound reciprocal dealing relationships between institutions and to render unconditional mutual assistance
C. to demonstrate the best ethical behavior in strict accordance with the content and spirit of The Model Code
D. to maintain the highest possible standards in their profession by constantly setting an example of propriety in business

Correct Answer: B Section: Volume C

QUESTION 191
Which of the following statements reflects the position of the Model Code on gambling or betting amongst market participants?

A. Gambling and betting amongst market participants should be strongly discouraged.
B. Gambling and betting amongst market participants may be permitted if management monitors it.

C. Gambling and betting amongst market participants should be prohibited.
D. Gambling and betting amongst market participants is only tolerated if it is previously reported to the CFP of the ACI.

Correct Answer: A Section: Volume C

QUESTION 192
The popularity of FX-trading via Internet platforms has serious implications for the applicability of traditional rules such as "Know Your Customer". Which of the following are correct?

A. "Know Your Customer" rules cannot be applied online and banks will have to rely instead on new safeguards such as third-party authentication.
B. "Know Your Customer" rules apply only to retail customers and are therefore irrelevant to currency trading.
C. In practice, banks can avoid "Know Your Customer" rules by limiting online deal size to EUR 100,000.00 or equivalent.
D. No trading should be carried out without first identifying and setting up the counterparty; this includes "Know Your Customer" procedures.

Correct Answer: D Section: Volume C

QUESTION 193
Where voicemail equipment is used for the reporting and recording of off-premises transactions, voice mail should be:

A. installed on secret number known only to the chief dealer
B. installed and located in the office of the head of compliance
C. installed and located in such a way that reported transactions cannot be subsequently erased without senior management approval.
D. securely saved by recordings that have to be stored for at least a twelve-month period

Correct Answer: C Section: Volume C

QUESTION 194
In a plain vanilla interest rate swap, the "fixed-rate payer":

A. has established the price sensitivities of a longer-term fixed-rate liability and a floating-rate asset
B. has established the price sensitivities of a longer-term fixed-rate asset and a floating-rate liability

C. receives fixed in the swap
D. pays floating in the swap

Correct Answer: A Section: Volume C

QUESTION 195
All prices quoted by brokers should be taken to be:

A. under reference
B. firm, but not necessarily in marketable amounts
C. firm, unless otherwise qualified
D. merely indicative

Correct Answer: C Section: Volume C

QUESTION 196
What should a broker do if his quoted price is hit simultaneously by several dealers for a total amount greater than that for which the price concerned was valid?

A. allot the amount for which the price is valid pro rata amongst some principals in accordance with the amount proposed by each and inform the other dealers that "nothing was done"
B. decide which principals he will allot the amount for which the price is valid and inform the other dealers that "nothing was done"
C. evenly allocate the amount for which the price is valid amongst all the principals and inform all the relevant dealers
D. apportion the amount for which the price is valid pro rata amongst all the principals concerned in accordance with the amount proposed by each and inform all the relevant dealers

Correct Answer: D Section: Volume C

QUESTION 197
Under the Model Code, if a broker shouts "done" or "mine" at the very moment a dealer shouts "off":

A. No deal is done and the broker should inform both counterparties accordingly.
B. The deal is done and the broker should inform both counterparties accordingly.
C. The matter should be resolved in consultation with senior management of the 3 institutions.
D. The ACI's Committee for Professionalism will investigate and advise accordingly.

Correct Answer: B Section: Volume C

QUESTION 198
In order to be introduced in a controlled manner, which areas should be involved before a new product or business strategy is launched?

A. Product Control, Legal and Compliance, Front Office, Treasury and Operations
B. Senior management only
C. Front Office and Treasury Middle Office
D. All relevant areas

Correct Answer: D Section: Volume C

QUESTION 199
Which of the following currencies is quoted on an ACT/365 basis for the calculation of interest on interbank deposits in London?

A. EUR
B. JPY
C. HKD
D. AUD

Correct Answer: C Section: Volume C

QUESTION 200
A negative yield curve is one in which:

A. Longer rates are lower than short rates
B. Forward exchange rates are at a discount
C. Short term rates are lower than long
D. Forward exchange rates are a premium

Correct Answer: A Section: Volume C

QUESTION 201
What is the day count/annual basis convention for JPY money market deposits?

A. ACT/365
B. ACT/360
C. ACT/ACT
D. 30E/360

Correct Answer: B Section: Volume C

QUESTION 202
What rates should a panel bank contribute to the EURIBOR fixings?

A. The offer side of the quotes it is making to other banks
B. The offer side of the quotes which it is receiving from other banks
C. The offer side of the interbank quotes it observes being made by prime banks
D. The offer side of the quotes it has actually borrowed at

Correct Answer: C Section: Volume C

QUESTION 203
EURIBOR is the:

A. Daily fixing of EUR interbank deposit rates in the European market
B. Daily fixing of EUR interbank deposit rates in the London market
C. Another name for EUR LIBOR
D. The ECB's official repo rate

Correct Answer: A Section: Volume C

QUESTION 204
A USD deposit traded in London between two German banks is cleared:

A. Wherever the parties agree
B. In London
C. In NewYork
D. In Frankfurt

Correct Answer: C Section: Volume C

QUESTION 205
If the issuer of the collateral used in a repo defaults during the term of the transaction, who suffers the loss?

A. Buyer
B. Seller
C. Issuer
D. It depends on the agreement between the buyer and seller

Correct Answer: B Section: Volume C

QUESTION 206
What is the Purchase Price of a repo?

A. The market value of bond collateral at the start of the repo at the clean price of the bond
B. The market value of bond collateral at the start of the repo at the dirty price of the bond
C. The amount of cash actually paid for collateral at the start of the repo
D. The amount of cash actually paid for collateral at the start of the repo plus repo interest

Correct Answer: C Section: Volume C

QUESTION 207
A CD with a face value of USD 250,000,000.00 was issued at par with a coupon of 5% for 91 days.

You buy it in the secondary market when it has 30 days remaining to maturity and is trading at 5.25%. How much do you pay?

A. USD 252,056,972.97
B. USD 252,028,916.32
C. USD 250,000,000.00
D. USD 248,911,014.31

Correct Answer: A Section: Volume C

QUESTION 208
All other things being equal, if a bank borrows short and lends long what is the effect on the liquidity risk of the bank?

A. positive
B. changes only when interest rates levels are high
C. negative
D. changes only when interest rates levels are low

Correct Answer: C Section: Volume D

QUESTION 209
A transaction that entails market price risks may be entered into in the absence of a market price risk limit...

A ..... only at the discretion of the head of treasury.
B ..... only at the discretion of the head of trading.
C ..... as long a counterparty and issuer limit is in place.
D ...... is not permitted.

Correct Answer: D Section: Volume D

QUESTION 210
The risk associated with a stock or a bond that is not correlated with events in the market is known as:

A. interest rate risk
B. model risk
C. currency risk
D. specific risk

Correct Answer: D Section: Volume D

QUESTION 211
What is the correct interpretation of a EUR 5,000,000.00 one-week VaR figure with a 99% confidence level?

A. A loss of at least EUR 5,000,000.00 can be expected in 99 out of the next 100 weeks.
B. A loss of at most EUR 5,000,000.00 can be expected in 1 out of the next 100 weeks.
C. A loss of at most EUR 5,000,000.00 can be expected in 1 out of the next 100 days.
D. A loss of at least EUR 5,000,000.00 can be expected in 1 out of the next 100 weeks.

Correct Answer: D Section: Volume D

QUESTION 212
Which one of the formulae below is correct?

A. Long a FRN + pay fixed on a swap = long a synthetic straight bond
B. Long a FRN + receive floating on a swap = long a synthetic straight bond
C. Long a FRN + pay floating on a swap = short a synthetic straight bond
D. Long a FRN + pay floating on a swap = long a synthetic straight bond.

Correct Answer: D Section: Volume D

QUESTION 213
A bank quotes 3-month EUR deposits at 0.45% ¡ª 0.55% to its broker. The broker lifts the bank's offer at 0.55%. Which of the following steps must the broker take?

A. The broker must show the borrower's name to the lender first and disclose the lender's name only if the borrower is acceptable to the lender.
B. The broker must show the lender's name to the borrower first and disclose the borrower's name only if the lender is acceptable to the borrower.
C. The broker must show the borrower's and lender's names to each other at the same time.
D. For marketing reasons, the broker can show the lender's name to the borrower at any time.

Correct Answer: A Section: Volume D

QUESTION 214
Where dealing for personal account is allowed, what safeguards to prevent abuse or insider dealing are stated by the Model Code?

A. The need to maintain confidentiality with respect to non-public price sensitive information
B. The maximum amounts or sizes of trades dealers are allowed to trade for their own account
C. The instruments/products dealers can trade for their own account
D. The pledge that no action is taken by employees that might adversely affect the interests of clients or counterparties

Correct Answer: B Section: Volume D

QUESTION 215
Principals are allowed to:

A. visit a broker's dealing room to arrange or confirm deals
B. visit a broker's dealing room with the permission of the management of both parties
C. deal from within a broker's dealing room with the permission of the broker's management
D. place an order with a broker from within the same broker's office

Correct Answer: B Section: Volume D

QUESTION 216
What needs to be done in the event that a trade is amended by one or both parties?

A. A new confirmation should be generated by both parties but there is no need to restart the confirmation cycle.
B. The amending party should verbally inform the other party.
C. A new confirmation should be generated and the confirmation cycle should restart and continue until the trade is completely matched by both parties.
D. A new confirmation need not be generated but the confirmation cycle must restart and continue until the trade is completely matched by both parties.

Correct Answer: C Section: Volume D

QUESTION 217
Management has a specific responsibility to issue guidelines to staff on transacting after-hours and off-premises. Which of the following does the Model Code suggest?

A. Dealing should only be allowed during normal trading hours.
B. It is not recommended that an unofficial close of business be specified for each trading day.
C. There should be clear written guidelines regarding the limit and type of deals that are permitted after normal hours or off-premises.
D. All after-hours and off-premises transactions must be dealt exclusively with the dealer's personal mobile phones

Correct Answer: C Section: Volume D

QUESTION 218
You have bought a 93-day US Treasury bill at 5.63%. What is the true yield?

A. 5.71%
B. 5.69%
C. 5.72%
D. 5.62%

Correct Answer: A Section: Volume D

QUESTION 219
When is interest conventionally due on a 3-year interbank EUR deposit?

A. At maturity
B. Annually
C. Semi-annually
D. Quarterly

Correct Answer: B Section: Volume D

QUESTION 220
The interest earned on a USD 5,000,000.oo money market deposit for 184 days is USD 12,500.00. What was the interest rate?

A. 0.470%
B. 0.196%
C. 0.500%
D. 0.169%

Correct Answer: D Section: Volume D

QUESTION 221
The buyer of a currency put option has:

A. Substantial opportunity for gain and limited risk of loss
B. Substantial risk of loss and substantial opportunity for gain
C. Limited risk of loss and limited opportunity for gain
D. Substantial risk of loss and limited opportunity for gain

Correct Answer: A Section: Volume D

QUESTION 222
The rho of an option is:

A. The sensitivity of the option value to changes in interest rates
B. The sensitivity of the option value to changes in volatility
C. The sensitivity of the option value to changes in the time to expiry
D. The sensitivity of the option value to changes in the price of the underlying

Correct Answer: A Section: Volume D

QUESTION 223
Which of the following statements regarding economic capital is correct?

A. Economic capital is calculated externally and is the amount of capital the firm should have to support its target credit rating
B. Economic capital is calculated on an expected shortfall basis with a specific time horizon and confidence level.
C. Economic capital is used for measuring and reporting risks across a financial organisation.
D. Economic capital is always lower than regulatory capital because of the more adequate modelling of correlation effects compared to the regulatory approach.

Correct Answer: C Section: Volume D

QUESTION 224
Who typically communicates the bank's asset and liability management policy internally?

A. the management board
B. the chief risk officer
C. the bank's ALCO
D. the Risk and Capital Committee

Correct Answer: C Section: Volume D

QUESTION 225
You have prepared the following economic capital table for the next ALCO meeting:

Credit risk:	minimum 100 ; maximum 200 ; actual 170
Interest rate risk:	minimum 10 ; maximum 20 ; actual 12
Liquidity risk:	minimum 5 ; maximum 10 ; actual 11
Currency risk:	minimum 5 ; maximum 10 ; actual 6

For which of the following risks should you consider actions?

A. credit risk
B. interest rate risk
C. liquidity risk
D. currency risk

Correct Answer: C Section: Volume D

QUESTION 226
All other things being equal the interest rate risk of a fixed coupon bond is:

A. greater, the higher the coupon and the longer the term
B. greater, the lower the coupon and the longer the term
C. lower, the lower the coupon and the shorter the term
D. lower, the higher the coupon and the longer the term

Correct Answer: B Section: Volume D

QUESTION 227
What is settlement risk in FX?

A. The risk of failure of a payments or settlement system
B. The risk that only one side of an exchange of currencies will be made
C. The risk of payments 'gridlock' in a real-time gross settlement system
D. The risk that default by a counterparty before the value date means you have to replace the defaulted deal at a worse rate

Correct Answer: B Section: Volume D

QUESTION 228
Taking collateral to hedge the credit risk on a counterparty means that you have:

A. Eliminated credit risk
B. Eliminated market risk
C. Taken a guarantee from the issuer of the collateral
D. Taken on market, legal and operational risks

Correct Answer: D Section: Volume D

QUESTION 229
You want to hedge your deposit against falling interest rates. Which of the alternatives below are appropriate for this purpose?

A. Selling a Money Market Future and/or selling a Forward Rate Agreement
B. Buying a Money Market Future and/or buying a Forward Rate Agreement
C. Selling a Money Market Future and/or buying a Forward Rate Agreement
D. Buying a Money Market Future and/or selling a Forward Rate Agreement

Correct Answer: D Section: Volume D

QUESTION 230
You are the fixed-rate payer in a plain vanilla interest rate swap. If your counterparty defaults, your exposure at default is:

A. greater, the higher the market swap rate and the shorter the term
B. lower, the lower the market swap rate and the shorter the term
C. lower, the lower the market swap rate and the longer the term
D. greater, the higher the market swap rate and the longer the term

Correct Answer: D Section: Volume D

QUESTION 231
Extended trading hours and off-premises dealing can involve additional hazards, the avoidance of which requires clear controls. The Model Code prescribes best market practice. Which of thefollowing is true?

A. Off-premises dealing should be strictly prohibited.
B. After-hours trading should be prohibited.
C. Deals transacted after normal business hours or off-premises should only be undertaken on mobile phones approved by management.
D. Deals transacted after normal business hours or off-premises either by mobile phones or any other equipment should only be undertaken with the approval of management.

Correct Answer: D Section: Volume D

QUESTION 232
What should be done when a voice broker calls "off" at the very instant the dealer hits the broker's price as "mine" or "yours"?

A. The transaction should be concluded and the broker should inform both counterparties accordingly.
B. The dealer who hits the broker's price may decide whether the deal is done or not; the broker should inform both counterparties accordingly.
C. The deal should not be concluded and the broker should inform both counterparties accordingly.
D. The broker should immediately inform both counterparties that the deal will have to berenegotiated.

Correct Answer: C Section: Volume D

QUESTION 233
Where there are shared management responsibilities or where an investment or shareholding exists in a broker by a counterparty:

A. the broker is not obligated to reveal any material connections provided Chinese Walls are in place.
B. the broker is not required to reveal any connections at all.
C. the broker is legally obliged to advise his clients of any material connections that exist.
D. is a matter which is not covered by the Model Code.

Correct Answer: C Section: Volume D

QUESTION 234
Dealers are authorized to deal:

A. anywhere, even away from their own dealing premises
B. after-hours, but only if listed as such by management
C. after-hours, but only from their private residence
D. away from their broker's dealing premises

Correct Answer: B Section: Volume D

QUESTION 235
Which of the following statements about "standard settlement instructions" (SSI) is correct?

A. The Head of Operations has the sole responsibility of ensuring the correctness and validity of the SSI setup.
B. SSIs should be stored and maintained in the bank's general static data system.
C. Each institution should have a separate SSI team to prevent I minimise the potential risk of fraud.
D. SSI staff should be fully integrated within Operations to insure consistent and reliable settlement guidelines.

Correct Answer: C Section: Volume D

QUESTION 236
Which of the following is a Model Code good practice regarding the passing of names?

A. Bank dealers should, wherever possible, give brokers prior indication of counterparties with whom they would be unwilling to do business.
B. Brokers may divulge the names of principals prematurely to induce a counterparty to transact.
C. Dealers should never give brokers guidance on the extent of their price differentiation across broad categories of counterparties.
D. When a principal's name proves unacceptable to another principal, the broker is bound to divulge who refused it.

Correct Answer: A Section: Volume D

QUESTION 237
Three of the following non-EU countries have unilaterally adopted the Euro. Which one has not?

A. Kosovo
B. Andorra
C. Albania
D. Montenegro

Correct Answer: C Section: Volume D

QUESTION 238
Which of the following is not an officially published settlement or reference rate?

A. LIBID
B. LIBOR
C. EURIBOR
D. EURO LIBOR

Correct Answer: A Section: Volume D

QUESTION 239
When a broker needs to switch a name this should be done:

A. only after consultation with the local regulator
B. only if the switching transaction is done at the current market rate
C. only provided that such transactions are identified as switching transactions
D. only after approval by the broker's senior management

Correct Answer: C Section: Volume D

QUESTION 240
Once a prime-broker has matched and accepted a trade, separate confirmations must be exchanged between:

A. the prime-broker and the executing dealer only
B. the prime-broker and the executing dealer, and between the executing dealer and the client
C. the prime-broker and the executing dealer, and between the prime-broker and the client
D. the prime-broker and the client, and between the executing dealer and the client

Correct Answer: C Section: Volume D

QUESTION 241
A fixed rate forward/forward non-deliverable deposit/loan transaction, settled in cash with an agreed upon process for calculating the market reference at the commencement of the forward/forward period, is called:

A. an interest rate swap
B. a forward rate agreement
C. a short term interest rate future
D. an interest rate collar

Correct Answer: B Section: Volume D

QUESTION 242
Convert 8.25% quoted on a semi-annually compounded money market basis for USD to the equivalent annually-compounded bond basis.

A. 8.30%
B. 8.52%
C. 8.54%
D. 8.69%

Correct Answer: C Section: Volume D

QUESTION 243
Today's date is Thursday 12th December. What is the spot value date? Assume no bank holidays.

A. 14th December
B. 15th December
C. 16th December
D. 17th December

Correct Answer: C Section: Volume D

QUESTION 244
Which of the following pays a return in the form of a discount to face value?

A. Treasury bill
B. CD
C. Interbank deposit
D. Classic repo

Correct Answer: A Section: Volume D

QUESTION 245
Which of the following will tend to have the lowest yield?

A. Interbank deposit
B. Certificate of deposit
C. Treasury bill
D. BA

Correct Answer: C Section: Volume D

QUESTION 246
Which of the following market participants would least likely be a user of repo?

A. Investment funds
B. Credit institutions and central banks
C. Corporates
D. Retail and private customers

Correct Answer: D Section: Volume D

QUESTION 247
When quoting the exchange rate between the USD and AUDI which is conventionally the base currency?

A. USD
B. AUD
C. Depends on whether the price is being quoted in Australia or the US
D. Depends on whether the price is being quoted interbank or to a customer

Correct Answer: B Section: Volume D

QUESTION 248
The buyer of a USD/ARS NDF could be:

A. a buyer of Argentine Pesos
B. expecting a falling USD/ARS rate
C. hedging against a weakening of the Argentine Peso
D. speculating on an appreciation of the Argentine Peso

Correct Answer: C Section: Volume D

QUESTION 249
A forward/forward FX swap:

A. is a contract by which the maturity of a regular FX swap can be extended at an historic (noncurrent) rate
B. is a swap transaction where the near leg is traded either value today or value tomorrow and the far leg is traded spot
C. is a swap that does not start spot and where both the near and the far leg are traded forward
D. is a transaction by which a maturing outright forward FX is prolonged at an historic (non-current) rate

Correct Answer: C Section: Volume D

QUESTION 250
If you have created a 'synthetic asset' by buying and selling a USD/CHF swap, what have you done?

A. Created an exposure to the CHF
B. Created an exposure to the USD
C. Switched a CI-IF asset temporarily into USD without taking currency risk
D. Switched a USD asset temporarily into CHF without taking currency risk

Correct Answer: C Section: Volume D

QUESTION 251
If I say that I have "bought and sold" EUR/USD in an FX swap, what have I done?

A. Bought EUR and sold USD spot, and sold EUR and bought USD forward
B. Bought USD and sold EUR spot, and sold USD and bought EUR forward

C. Synthetically taken a USD loan in exchange for making a EUR loan with the same counterparty
D. Sold EUR/USD spot and bought back EUR/USD forward

Correct Answer: A Section: Volume D

QUESTION 252
If EUR/USD is 1.3025-28 and the 6-month swap is 15.50/17, what is the 6-month outright price? A. 1.3042-1.30435

B. 1.30405-1.3045
C. 1.30095-1.3011
D. 1.4575- 1.4728

Correct Answer: B Section: Volume D

QUESTION 253
If spot USD/HKD is 7.7600 and USD/SGD is 1.2350, what is SGD/HKD?

A. 9.5836
B. 6.2834
C. 0.1591
D. 0.1043

Correct Answer: B Section: Volume D

QUESTION 254
If USD/JPY is quoted to you as 98.10-15 and USD/CHF as 0.9294-99, what is the rate at which you can buy CHF against JPY?

A. 105.50
B. 105.61
C. 10555
D. 0.009474

Correct Answer: B Section: Volume D

QUESTION 255
The market is quoting:

1-month (31-day) NOK   1.75¡ăk 3-month (91-day) NOK   2.05%

What is the 1x3 rate in NOK? A. 4.261%
B. 2.202%
C. 1.900%
D. 1.592%

Correct Answer: B Section: Volume D

QUESTION 256
The major difference between FRAs and futures is that FRAs are:

A. Exchange-traded
B. Margined
C. Standardized
D. Dealtoverthe counter

Correct Answer: D Section: Volume D

QUESTION 257
An FX forward outright has been dealt for a value date which is subsequently declared to be a bank holiday. According to the Model Code, the exchange rate for the deal:

A. should be adjusted to take account of the change in value date
B. cannot be adjusted if one of the counterparties wishes to adjust the rate but the other wishes to keep the original rate
C. must be adjusted if one of the counterparties wishes to adjust the rate but the other wishes to keep the original rate
D. should be adjusted if the adjustment is for two days or longer but not if it is for only one day

Correct Answer: A Section: Volume E

QUESTION 258
Under what conditions can an FX broker act as a position taker?

A. if a principal refuses to honour the deal
B. no conditions are required; the broker is entitled to take positions
C. only if he can not find another counterparty for a name switching
D. brokers act only as intermediaries or arrangers of deals

Correct Answer: D Section: Volume E

QUESTION 259
A prime broker may not reject a trade given up if:

A. the trade is not within the specified tenor limits
B. the trade is not within the specified credit limits
C. the trade details provided by the executing dealer and the client match
D. the trade is a permitted transaction type as specified in the give-up agreement with the executing dealer

Correct Answer: D Section: Volume E

QUESTION 260
Is gambling or betting between market participants allowed?

A. Yes, it is allowed for sporting events.
B. Yes, it is allowed if no money is involved.
C. Although not prohibited, it is strongly discouraged.
D. It is allowed for purposes of charity.

Correct Answer: C Section: Volume E

QUESTION 261
What is a "normal" shaped curve?

A. Gradual positive slope
B. Steep positive slope
C. Flat
D. Inverted

Correct Answer: A Section: Volume E

QUESTION 262
If you take an 18-month USD deposit, when is interest payable?

A. Quarterly
B. At maturity
C. Semi-annually
D. After one year and at maturity

Correct Answer: D Section: Volume E

QUESTION 263
Which of the following will tend to have the higher yield?

A. Treasury bill
B. Repo against Treasury bill collateral
C. They have the same yield
D. Cannot say

Correct Answer: B Section: Volume E

QUESTION 264
What type of risk would describe the failure of a back office to make adequate margin calls on repo positions?

A. Credit risk
B. Market risk
C. Operational risk
D. Settlement risk

Correct Answer: C Section: Volume E

QUESTION 265
Which one of the following statements concerning covenants is incorrect?

A. Covenants are clauses in bank credit agreements and bond indentures designed to assure debt holders that the creditworthiness of the borrower(s)/issuer(s) will remain satisfactory
B. Covenants must be tailored to reflect the specific needs of the borrower/issuer and the specific risks perceived by the debt holders.
C. Covenants require the holder of the debt to refrain from doing certain specific things.
D. Three different types of covenants in credit agreements and bond indentures are affirmative, negative and financial.

Correct Answer: C Section: Volume E

QUESTION 266
Under Basel rules, what is the meaning of LGD?

A. Loss Given Default
B. Liquidity Given Distress
C. Limit Given Default
D. Loss Given Distress

Correct Answer: A Section: Volume E

QUESTION 267
What do you call a combination of a long (short) call option and short (long) put option with same face value, same expiration date, same style, where the strike price is equal to the forward price?

A. a synthetic forward
B. a straddle
C. risk reversal
D. a strangle

Correct Answer: A Section: Volume E

QUESTION 268
Which one of the following is a major objective of ACI-The Financial Markets Association?

A. to promote globalization and deregulation of the financial markets
B. to maintain the professional level of competence and to disseminate a high level of ethical and professional behavior
C. to act as the official international market regulator in the absence of government regulation
D. to become the sole global corporation of wholesale financial market professionals

Correct Answer: B Section: Volume E

QUESTION 269
When may a broker assume a deal is closed?

A. When one of the principals confirms the deal
B. When the principals give a written undertaking for all deals done at the end of the day
C. When acknowledgement is received from the principals that the deal is done
D. When both back offices acknowledge the deal

Correct Answer: C Section: Volume E

QUESTION 270
What is the recommended follow-up procedure in case of a settlement discrepancy?

A. All investigation cases should be handled within the same day
B. All investigation cases should be handled within 2 days
C. Investigation cases received before noon should be handled within the same day and those received after midday should be handled before noon the next day
D. Investigation cases received before noon should be handled within the same day and those received after midday within 24 hours

Correct Answer: C Section: Volume E

QUESTION 271
In dealing terminology, what does "my risk" refer to?

A. the market amount for which the quote is valid
B. the acknowledgement by the broker that he may be stuffed
C. the acknowledgement by the dealer receiving the quote that the rate may have to be re-quoted
D. the quoting dealer cautions the receiver of the quote that the price may have to be re-quoted at the receiver's risk

Correct Answer: A Section: Volume E

QUESTION 272
Which one of the following statements about "CLS rescinds" is correct?

A. CLS settlement members may rescind instructions unilaterally provided that the rescind messages reach the CLS Bank before the 00:00 CET deadline.
B. CLS settlement members may rescind instructions unilaterally provided that the rescind messages reach the CLS Bank before the 06:30 CET deadline.
C. CLS settlement members may rescind instructions bilaterally only if the rescind messages reach the CLS Bank before the 00:00 CET deadline.
D. CLS settlement members may rescind instructions bilaterally only if the rescind messages reach the CLS Bank after the 06:30 CET deadline.

Correct Answer: A Section: Volume E

QUESTION 273
The process of confirming trades is a function that can be performed by:

A. any dealer as long as he/she is not a party to the trade
B. staff in the back-office/operations who are independent of the trade
C. staff in the dealing room who are not dealing
D. any staff outside the dealing room

Correct Answer: B Section: Volume E

QUESTION 274
Your broker quotes you EUR/USD at 1.3425-28. You respond by saying "yours". Which one of the following statements is true?

A. You are committed to sell a marketable EUR amount unless the quote was for a specific amount.
B. You are committed to sell to the counterparty his full EUR amount subject to credit limits on the counterparty.
C. You are committed to sell EUR up to the amount permitted by your credit limits on the counterparty.
D. You are committed to sell a marketable USD amount unless the quote was for a specific amount.

Correct Answer: A Section: Volume E

QUESTION 275
Which SWIFT message should be used to advise the netting position of a currency resulting from FX, NDF, options and other trades?

A. MTn99
B. MT300
C. MT370
D. MT670/671

Correct Answer: C Section: Volume E

QUESTION 276
What does the Model Code advise regarding the taping of telephone conversations?

A. The tapes and other records should be kept until the transaction has been settled
B. Firms should ensure that they comply with local privacy laws

C. Management should ensure that the installation and control of recording equipment complies with local legislation, including laws on data protection, privacy and human rights as well as the manufacturers minimum requirements
D. All front office personnel should have access to these tapes and records

Correct Answer: B Section: Volume E

ENG012-8th

QUESTION 277
From the following CAD rates:

1M (31-day) CAD deposit   0.95%
1x2 CAD (30-day) FRA   1.21%
2x3 CAD (31-day) FRA   2.01%

Calculate the 3-month implied cash rate.

A. 1.42%
B. 1.39%
C. 2.01%
D. 4.21%

Correct Answer: B
Section: Volume E

QUESTION 278
Using the following rates:

3M (90-day) EUR deposit   0.25%
6M (180-day) EUR deposit   0.50%

What is the rate for a EUR deposit, which runs from 3 to 6 months? A. 0.25%
B. 0.375%
C. 0.75%
D. 0.50%

Correct Answer: C Section: Volume E

QUESTION 279
The two-week repo rate for the 5.25% Bund 2011 is quoted to you at 3.33-38%. You agree to reverse in bonds worth EUR 266,125,000.00, but insist on an initial margin of 2%. You would earn repo interest of:

A. EUR 337,874A0
B. EUR 342,947.58
C. EUR 337,739.24
D. EUR 342,810.40

Correct Answer: A Section: Volume E

QUESTION 280
What is an outright forward FX transaction?

A. A spot sale (purchase) and a forward purchase (sale)
B. A spot sale (purchase) and a forward sale (purchase)
C. An exchange of currencies on a date beyond spot and at a price fixed today
D. An exchange of currencies on a date beyond spot

Correct Answer: C Section: Volume E

QUESTION 281
If a 12-month AUD/NZD swap is quoted 53/47, which of the following statements would you consider to be correct?

A. 12-month AUD rates are higher than 12-month NZD rates
B. 12-month AUD rates are lower than 12-month NZD rates
C. Spot AUD/NZD will be higher by approximately 50 points in 12 months
D. The AUD yield curve is positive, whilst the NZD curve is negative

Correct Answer: A Section: Volume E

QUESTION 282
You wish to sell a customer GBP/USD for value tomorrow. How can you hedge yourself?

A. Sell and buy GBP/USD T/N
B. Buy and sell GBP/USD T/N
C. Sell GBP/USD spot, and sell and buy GBP/USD T/N
D. Buy GBP/USD spot, and buy and sell GBP/USD T/N

Correct Answer: D Section: Volume E

QUESTION 283
You are quoted the following rates:

Spot USD/JPY   97.10-15
3M USD/JPY swap   9/6   Spot USD/CHF   0932-23
3M USD/CHF swap   11/8

Where can you sell CHF against JPY 3-month outright?

A. 104.14
B. 104.21
C. 104.23
D. 104.30

Correct Answer: A Section: Volume E

QUESTION 284
If a dealer needs to hedge an over-lent 3x6 position against 1MM dates for which the FRA is quoted 1.30-1.34% and futures at 98.64, which would be cheapest for him (ignoring margin costs on futures positions) to cover his gap?

A. FRA
B. Futures
C. No difference
D. Too little information to decide

Correct Answer: A Section: Volume E

QUESTION 285
The delta of an 'at-the-money' long call option is:

A. Between +0.5 and +1
B. +0.5
C. Between 0 and +0.5
D. Zero

Correct Answer: B
Section: Volume E

QUESTION 286
A long collar is:

A. A purchase of a cap and a sale of a floor
B. A purchase of a floor and a sale of a cap
C. A purchase of a cap and a purchase of a floor
D. A sale of a cap and a sale of a floor

Correct Answer: A Section: Volume E

QUESTION 287
What is the purpose of the Liquidity Coverage Ratio?

A. to mitigate market replacement risk across markets
B. to eliminate funding mismatches by establishing a minimum acceptable amount of stable funding
C. to ensure that banks have enough high-quality liquid assets to survive a 30-day period of acute market stress
D. to minimize duration risk on a bank's assets over a one-year horizon

Correct Answer: C Section: Volume E

QUESTION 288
Which of the following is a measure of a bank's gross exposure to foreign exchange rate risk?

A. The maturity mismatch among assets and liabilities denominated in the home and reporting currencies.
B. The gap between variable and fixed rate assets and liabilities across all currencies.
C. The sum of all assets in one currency minus the sum of all liabilities in that same currency.
D. The sum of all off-balance sheet assets in one foreign currency minus the on-balance sheet equity in another currency.

Correct Answer: C Section: Volume E

QUESTION 289
When constructing a gap report, how would a EUR 25,000,000.00 long position in 6x12 FRA be categorized?

A. as a EUR 25,000,000.00 6-month liability and a EUR 25,000,000.00 12-month asset
B. as a EUR 25,000,000.00 12-month liability and a EUR 25,000,000.00 6-month asset
C. as a EUR 12,500,000.00 6-month liability and a EUR 12,500,000.00 12-month asset
D. as a EUR 12,500,000.00 6-month asset and a EUR 12,500,000.00 12-month liability

Correct Answer: B Section: Volume E

QUESTION 290
What would happen to a bank's net interest income if it ran a zero gap in an environment of decreasing interest rates?

A. Net interest income would increase slightly.
B. Net interest income would increase considerably.
C. Net interest income would decrease.
D. Net interest income would hardly change at all.

Correct Answer: D Section: Volume E

QUESTION 291
What is a hedge?

A. A means by which to reduce a risk
B. An equal and opposite risk
C. A riskless transaction
D. A means of cancelling a deal

Correct Answer: A Section: Volume E

QUESTION 292
When is your settlement risk greatest on a spot FX deal?

A. Today
B. Tomorrow
C. After you make an irrevocable payment
D. On the spot value date

Correct Answer: C Section: Volume E

QUESTION 293
Which of the following is a characteristic of all liquid assets under Basel III?

A. uncertainty of valuation
B. high correlation with risky assets
C. listed on a developed and recognized exchange
D. readily marketable
Correct Answer: D Section: Volume E

QUESTION 294
Today, you sell GBP 5,000,000.00 to a customer against JPY for spot value. Tomorrow, the customer defaults. What is your exposure called?

A. Replacement risk
B. Settlement risk
C. Legal risk
D. Basis risk
Correct Answer: A Section: Volume E

QUESTION 295
Which one of the following best describes expected shortfall/conditional value-at-risk at the 95% level?

A. the expected loss on the portfolio in the worst 95% of cases
B. the expected loss in those cases where the loss exceeds the VaR at the 95% level
C. the maximum loss in those cases where the loss exceeds the VaR at the 95% level
D. the expected loss in those cases where the loss exceeds the VaR at the 5% level

Correct Answer: B Section: Volume E

QUESTION 296
For a bank to count funds as regulatory capital:

A. There has to be an ultra long term maturity date
B. The risk taken by the bank must be taken or shared by provider of the capital
C. The funds must be in the form of pure equity
D. The funds must be re-invested only in cash
Correct Answer: B Section: Volume E

QUESTION 297
In FX trading a "third party beneficiary" is best described as:

A. the issuer of a payment for the relevant trade distinct from the counterparty
B. the issuer of a payment for the relevant trade identical to the counterparty
C. the recipient of a payment for the relevant trade distinct from the counterparty
D. the recipient of a payment for the relevant trade identical to the counterparty

Correct Answer: C Section: Volume E

QUESTION 298
If manual trade capture methods are used, when should deals be recorded in systems used for this purpose?

A. The same day they are dealt
B. Promptly
C. Within 24 hours of execution
D. Within an hour of execution

Correct Answer: B Section: Volume E

QUESTION 299
Between which departments are clear and structured escalation procedures required for the management of incorrect funding balances?

A. Nostro reconciliations, the Cash Management Department and Operations
B. Front Office, the Cash Management Department and Operations
C. Front Office, Nostro reconciliations and Operations
D. Front Office, Nostro reconciliations and the Cash Management Department

Correct Answer: B Section: Volume E

QUESTION 300
A bank quotes a spot rate that is verifiably incorrect and deviates substantially from the prevailing market rate.

A. you should hit the price and hold the bank to the quoted incorrect rate, as the quoted party is entitled to hold the quoting party to an erroneous

rate
- B. you should ask the dealer to check his price, as it is highly unethical for one party to hold another to an erroneously agreed rate
- C. you should point out the mistake and split the difference
- D. you should keep on dealing with this bank until the mistake is rectified

Correct Answer: B
Section: Volume E

QUESTION 301
In foreign exchange markets, the first currency in a currency pair is:

- A. The quoted currency
- B. The base currency
- C. The counter currency
- D. The terms currency

Correct Answer: B **Section: Volume E**

QUESTION 302
Which of the following statements is an incorrect statement in respect of Model Code recommendations concerning electronic trading?

- A. It is recommended that ECNs have mechanisms that control price flashing
- B. A manual kill button that disables the system's ability to trade and cancels all resting orders may not be established without Central Bank approval
- C. The sudden withdrawal of a specific credit limit or limits in a tactical manipulation to mislead the market is unethical
- D. Algorithms require appropriate supervision performed by staff with commensurate levels of experience

Correct Answer: B **Section: Volume E**

QUESTION 303
What are financial market professionals not explicitly required by the Model Code to clarify and agree to in writing?

- A. that the customer understands he will be charged for advisory services that are provided
- B. that the customer understands the terms, conditions and risks of the transaction

C. that the customer understands that any information or should not be interpreted as investment advice or recommendations
D. that the customer understands he is entering into the transaction at his own risk and for his own account.

Correct Answer: A Section: Volume E

QUESTION 304
When should confirmations be sent out?

A. one day after the deal is done
B. within two hours of the trade being booked and as soon as technologically possible
C. immediately after having received the confirmation of the counterparty
D. no later than the value date of the first leg of the transaction

Correct Answer: B Section: Volume E

QUESTION 305
In the unforeseen event that a particular maturity date is declared a public holiday, what is standard market practice for spot FX?

A. to extend the contract to the next business day
B. to shorten the contract to the previous business day
C. The two parties involved agree to a new maturity date.
D. There is no standard market practice. ACIs Committee for Professionalism decides the issue on a case-by-case basis.

Correct Answer: A Section: Volume E

QUESTION 306
What should a dealer say to express his commitment to putting an additional bid or offer at a current bid or offer price already quoted by his broker?

A. same way"
B. me too"
C. "par", or "parity"
D. "join at", or "support at"

Correct Answer: D Section: Volume E

QUESTION 307
If making a claim in respect of "use of funds", payments should be settled within how many days?

A. 15
B. 20
C. 35
D. 40

Correct Answer: C Section: Volume E

QUESTION 308
Which of following terms is not used as an expression for dates other than regular dates/periods?

A. cock dates
B. broken dates
C. odd dates
D. weird dates

Correct Answer: D Section: Volume E

QUESTION 309
Which of the following statements with respect to trading and broking ethics through the use of technology is the correct quote from the Model Code?

A. Deliberate attempts at gaming and abuse using the flashing of orders without the intent to deal should be classified as proprietary trades.
B. Management should ensure that the complete e-trading process, from pricing to risk impact through to settlement, conforms to recognized standards and market conventions.
C. All bid-offers presented to electronic platforms should remain in the Matching System for no more than the minimum period of time defined within their respective Minimum Quote Life (MQL) rules.
D. Trades which occur at off-market rates, by agreement between the two counterparts and as soon as practically possible, should stand and any profit be equitably divided between them.

Correct Answer: B Section: Volume E

QUESTION 310
The Model Code is clear on "position parking". What does it say?

A. The parking of deals or positions with any counterparty is discouraged
B. The parking of deals or positions with any counterparty should be forbidden
C. The parking of deals or positions should be subject to a clear policy laid down in writing by senior management
D. In jurisdictions where position parking is allowed, prior approval should be sought from the regulator

Correct Answer: B Section: Volume E

QUESTION 311
Which of the following statements about Eurodollar deposits is correct?

A. Eurodollar deposits can only be dealt by banks in the USA
B. US withholding tax applies to Eurodollar deposits
C. Eurodollar deposits are free of US reserve requirements
D. Eurodollar deposits are subject to US exchange controls

Correct Answer: C Section: Volume E

QUESTION 312
A CD can usually only be issued by what type of institution?

A. Credit institution
B. Investment bank
C. Discount house
D. Corporate

Correct Answer: A Section: Volume E

QUESTION 313
If the value of the collateral in a repo has fallen during the term of the transaction, who suffers the loss?

A. Seller
B. Buyer
C. Issuer
D. It depends on the agreement between the buyer and seller

Correct Answer: A Section: Volume E

QUESTION 314
What does the Model Code recommend with regard to any give-up agreement between a prime broker and an executing dealer?

A. That the Master FX Give-Up Agreement (FMLG - New York FED FXC) published by the Foreign Exchange Committee can be used for this purpose.
B. That this agreement need not specify the permitted transaction types, tenors or credit limits.
C. That this agreement must include instructions that the prime broker must advise the executing dealer promptly of trades for give-up.
D. That this agreement should not involve any requirement for the executing dealer to inform the prime broker of the material terms of the transaction once a trade has been executed.

Correct Answer: A Section: Volume F

QUESTION 315
When initially negotiating an interest rate swap, a principal indicated his intention to assign it to a third party. In executing such a transfer:

A. The principal is entitled to provide the name of the original counterparty to the transferee.
B. The principal is entitled to provide the name of the transferee to the original counterparty.
C. The principal should obtain the consent of the transferee before releasing its name.
D. The principal should obtain the consent of the original counterparty before releasing its name to the transferee.

Correct Answer: C Section: Volume F

QUESTION 316
When an employee executes a personal trade in advance of a client's or institution's order to benefit from the anticipated movement in the market price following the execution of a large trade, it is called:

A. front running
B. ex ante trading
C. insider dealing
D. forward-facing

Correct Answer: A Section: Volume F

QUESTION 317
Dealers are allowed to trade for their own account only if:

A. they have good track records in dealing both for their institution and for themselves
B. there have been no previous conflicts of interest in the dealing room
C. there is a clearly defined and written policy about the matter
D. the dealers see no conflict of interest in such dealing

Correct Answer: C Section: Volume F

QUESTION 318
What does the Model Code recommend regarding the practice of "name switching/substitution"?

A. Dealers may seek a compensation payment in favor of the bank or an adjustment to brokerage bills from the broker for switching names.
B. If requested by a broker to clear a transaction through name switching, a dealer must ensure that such activities have the prior approval of senior management.
C. The practice of name switching/substitution is neither acceptable nor desirable.
D. Name switching/substitution transactions should be executed as promptly as possible not considering credit limits and policy guidelines.

Correct Answer: B Section: Volume F

QUESTION 319
If there is a need for assistance to help resolve a dispute over differences between a broker and a bank, the Model Code suggests turning to:

A. the monetary authority in the country where the broker is located
B. the banking association in the country where the bank is located
C. the Committee for Professionalism of the ACI
D. the local foreign exchange market committee

Correct Answer: C Section: Volume F

QUESTION 320
In spite of having agreed to a deal, dealers are not bound to its terms if it is "subject to documentation". What position does the Model Code take with regard to this practice?

A. The practice of making a transaction subject to documentation is not

regarded as good practice.
B. It urges dealers to be bear in mind that this is a common practice for capital market deals.
C. The Model Code does not comment on the matter.
D. It recommends that national ACI Associations deal with this issue according to their local customs.

Correct Answer: A

Section: Volume F

QUESTION 321
What recommendation does the Model Code make in cases of market disruption?

A. Market participants should strictly adhere to the rules issued by local regulators, supervisors or central banks in order to maintain efficiency and avoid disputes.
B. Even if local provisions are in place, market participants should only adhere to the ACI best practices of the Model Code in order to maintain efficiency and avoid disputes.
C. Participants must at all times adhere to the rules issued by local regulators, supervisors or central banks even if these rules or procedures conflict with any provision of an existing written agreement.
D. Parties may unilaterally decide whether they wish to adhere to the terms of the agreement or to amend the terms of the transaction to follow the relevant procedure.

Correct Answer: A Section: Volume F

QUESTION 322
What are 1MM dates?

A. the tenth of the following months: March, June, September and December
B. the third Wednesday of January, April, July and October
C. the Monday before the third Wednesday of March, June, September and December
D. the third Wednesday of March, June, September and December

Correct Answer: D Section: Volume F

QUESTION 323
A 3-month (91-day) UK Treasury bill with a face value of GBP 50,000,000.00 is quoted at a yield of 4.25%. How much is the bill worth?

A. GBP 47,875,000.00
B. GBP 49,462,847.22
C. GBP 49,470,205.48
D. GBP 49,475,760.27

Correct Answer: D Section: Volume F

QUESTION 324
Which of the following are quoted in terms of a discount rate?

A. US Treasury bill
B. CD
C. Interbank deposit
D. ECP

Correct Answer: A Section: Volume F

QUESTION 325
In case of a default on a repo by the seller:

A. The buyer can liquidate the collateral
B. The buyer has to liquidate the collateral
C. The buyer cannot liquidate the collateral until the seller is declared insolvent
D. A court is appointed to decide what happens to the collateral

Correct Answer: A Section: Volume F

QUESTION 326
On fixing date, the settlement payment of an NDF reflects the differential between the agreed forward rate and:

A. the fixing spot rate
B. the daily high
C. the days' average rate
D. the average rate over the NDF period

Correct Answer: A Section: Volume F

QUESTION 327
If EUR/USD is quoted to you as 1.3030-40 and GBP/USD as 1.5320-30, at what rate can you sell GBP and buy EUR?

A. 0.8500
B. 0.8506
C. 0.8512
D. 0.8505

Correct Answer: C Section: Volume F

QUESTION 328
When performing a gap analysis, into which of the following time buckets should a 5-year floating-rate note with a 6-month LIBOR coupon be slotted?

A. the 6-month bucket
B. the 2.5-year bucket
C. the 5-year bucket
D. It should be weighted and apportioned in each of the time buckets in accord with the periodic coupon payments.

Correct Answer: A Section: Volume F

QUESTION 329
Risk capital is intended to ensure that an institution can:

A. Survive a liquidity crisis
B. Absorb credit losses
C. Absorb any type of unexpected loss
D. Absorb any type of expected loss

Correct Answer: C Section: Volume F

QUESTION 330
You have just sold USD 5,000,000.00 spot against JPY. What type of risk does not apply?

A. Market risk
B. Settlement risk
C. Basis risk
D. Credit risk

Correct Answer: C Section: Volume F

QUESTION 331
If the daily 90% confidence level VaR of a portfolio is correctly estimated to be USD 5,000.00, one would expect that:

A. in 1 out of 10 days, the portfolio value will decline by USD 5,000.00 or less.
B. in 1 out of 90 days, the portfolio value will decline by USD 5,000.00 or less.
C. in 1 out of 10 days, the portfolio value will decline by USD 5,000.00 or more.
D. in 1 out of 90 days, the portfolio value will decline by USD 5,000.00 or more.

Correct Answer: C Section: Volume F

QUESTION 332
Which of the following definitions of a nostro account is correct?

A. A nostro account is an account held by a bank in a foreign country in the banks domestic currency.
B. A nostro account is an account held by a bank in a foreign country for cash collateralising OTC derivative positions with banks in that country.
C. A nostro account is an account held by a bank in a foreign country in the currency of that country.
D. A nostro account is an account held by a bank in its home country in a foreign currency.

Correct Answer: C Section: Volume F

QUESTION 333
Under Basel rules, what is the meaning of IRB?

A. Internal Risk Based
B. Internal Ratings Based
C. Intrinsic Risk Based
D. Internal Rule Based

Correct Answer: B Section: Volume F

QUESTION 334
Which position below is NOT a component of common equity Tier 1 capital?

A. innovative hybrid capital instruments with incentives to redeem
B. common shares issued by bank
C. retained earnings
D. stock surplus (share premium)

Correct Answer: A Section: Volume F

QUESTION 335
With reference to dealing periods, what does the term "short dates" refer to?

A. overnight, tom-next and spot-next
B. maturities up to one week
C. maturity dates of less than one month
D. maturity dates of less than 10 days

Correct Answer: C Section: Volume F

QUESTION 336
Which of the following statements is false? The repo legal agreement between the two parties concerned should:

A. enable the parties to comply with any capital adequacy requirements
B. provide for the absolute transfer of title to securities
C. provide for the calculation of initial consideration of the repo transaction
D. detail the course of action in the case of defaults, for example the rights and obligations of the counterparties and the full set-off of claims between the parties

Correct Answer: C Section: Volume F

QUESTION 337
An option granted by the seller that gives the buyer the right to enter into an underlying interest rate swap transaction is ca lied:

A. a swap
B. a cap
C. a swaption
D. a collar

Correct Answer: C Section: Volume F

QUESTION 338
What rate should be used if the settlement date in a foreign exchange transaction is no longer a "good" date?

A. The original rate of the transaction
B. The original rate of the transaction adjusted by the relevant forward points
C. The affected parties should agree to adjust the exchange rate according to the prevailing relevant forward mid swap points at the time the bank holiday is announced
D. The rate is open to negotiation by the two parties

Correct Answer: C Section: Volume F

QUESTION 339
How many USD would you have to invest at 3.5% to be repaid USD125 million (principal plus interest) in 30 days?

INTEREST RATE CONVERSIONS

Converting between bond basis and money market basis (Act/360)

$$rate_{bond\ basis} = rate_{money\ market\ basis} \cdot \frac{365}{360}$$

$$rate_{money\ market\ basis} = rate_{bond\ basis} \cdot \frac{360}{365}$$

Converting between annually and semi-annually compounding frequencies

$$rate_{annually\text{-}compounded} = \left(1 + \frac{rate_{semi\text{-}annually\ compounded}}{2}\right)^2 - 1$$

$$rate_{semi\text{-}annually\ compounded} = \left(\sqrt{1 + rate_{annually\ compounded}} - 1\right) \cdot 2$$

The formulae for converting between annually and semi-annually compounded rate apply only to rates quoted on a bond basis, not a money market basis.

MONEY MARKET

Certificates of deposit

$$\text{proceeds at maturity} = \text{face value}\left(1 + \frac{\text{coupon} \times \text{term}}{\text{annual basis}}\right)$$

$$\text{secondary market proceeds} = \frac{\text{proceeds at maturity}}{1 + \dfrac{\text{yield} \times \text{day count}}{\text{annual basis}}}$$

Discount-paying instruments quoted as a true yield

$$\text{secondary market proceeds} = \frac{\text{face value}}{1 + \dfrac{\text{yield} \times \text{day count}}{\text{annual basis}}}$$

Discount-paying instruments quoted as a rate of discount

$$\text{discount amount} = \text{face value} \, \frac{\text{rate of discount} \times \text{day count}}{\text{annual basis}}$$

$$\text{secondary market proceeds} = \text{face value}\left(1 - \frac{\text{rate of discount} \times \text{day count}}{\text{annual basis}}\right)$$

$$\text{true yield} = \frac{\text{rate of discount}}{1 - \dfrac{\text{rate of discount} \times \text{day count}}{\text{annual basis}}}$$

Forward price of sell/buy-back

$$\text{forward price} = \frac{(\text{repurchase price} - \text{accrued interest on collateral at termination})}{\text{nominal price of collateral}} \times 100$$

FORWARD-FORWARDS & FORWARD RATE AGREEMENTS

$$\text{forward - forward rate} = \left[\frac{1 + \dfrac{\text{interest rate}_{\text{long period}} \times \text{day count}_{\text{long period}}}{\text{annual basis}}}{1 + \dfrac{\text{interest rate}_{\text{short period}} \times \text{day count}_{\text{short period}}}{\text{annual basis}}} - 1\right] \frac{\text{annual basis}}{\text{day count}_{\text{forward-forward period}}}$$

$$\text{FRA settlement amount} = \text{notional principal amount} \frac{\left(\dfrac{(\text{FRA rate} - \text{settlement rate}) \times \text{day count}}{\text{annual basis}}\right)}{\left(1 + \dfrac{\text{settlement rate} \times \text{day count}}{\text{annual basis}}\right)}$$

$$\text{price} = 100\left[\left(\frac{\text{coupon}}{\text{yield}}\left(1-\frac{1}{(1+\text{yield})^{\text{remaining coupons}}}\right)\right)+\frac{1}{(1+\text{yield})^{\text{remaining coupons}}}\right]$$

Dirty price of bond with annual coupons

$$\text{dirty price} = \frac{\text{first cashflow}}{(1+\text{yield})^{\frac{\text{days to next coupon}}{\text{annual basis}}}} + \frac{\text{second cashflow}}{(1+\text{yield})^{1+\frac{\text{days to next coupon}}{\text{annual basis}}}} + \wedge + \frac{n^{\text{th}}\ \text{cashflow}}{(1+\text{yield})^{(n-1)+\frac{\text{days to next coupon}}{\text{annual basis}}}}$$

Duration at issue or on a coupon date

$$\text{Macaulay Duration} = \frac{\begin{bmatrix}(\text{present value of first coupon amount} \times \text{time to first coupon}) + \\ (\text{present value of second coupon amount} \times \text{time to second coupon}) + \ldots \\ + (\text{present value of }(\text{last coupon amount} + \text{nominal amount}) \times \text{time to last coupon})\end{bmatrix}}{\text{net present value of bond}}$$

$$\text{Modified Duration} = \frac{\text{Macaulay Duration}}{\left(1+\frac{\text{yield}}{\text{compounding frequency}}\right)}$$

Calculating zero-coupon yield from an annual yield-to-maturity (bootstrapping)

$$\text{zero-coupon yield for n-year term} = \left(\sqrt[n]{\frac{\text{final coupon amount} + \text{nominal amount}}{\text{implied present value of final coupon and nominal amount}}} - 1\right)100$$

FOREIGN EXCHANGE

Forward FX rate

$$\text{forward rate} = \text{spot rate} \times \frac{1 + \dfrac{\text{interest rate}_{\text{quoted currency}} \times \text{day count}}{\text{annual basis}_{\text{quoted currency}}}}{1 + \dfrac{\text{interest rate}_{\text{base currency}} \times \text{day count}}{\text{annual basis}_{\text{base currency}}}}$$

Covered interest arbitrage

synthetic quoted currency interest rate =

$$\left[\left(\left(1 + \frac{\text{interest rate}_{\text{base currency}} \times \text{day count}}{\text{annual basis}_{\text{base currency}}}\right) \frac{\text{forward rate}}{\text{spot rate}}\right) - 1\right] \frac{\text{annual basis}_{\text{quoted currency}}}{\text{day count}}$$

synthetic base currency interest rate =

$$\left[\left(\left(1 + \frac{\text{interest rate}_{\text{quoted currency}} \times \text{day count}}{\text{annual basis}_{\text{quoted currency}}}\right) \frac{\text{spot rate}}{\text{forward rate}}\right) - 1\right] \frac{\text{annual basis}_{\text{base currency}}}{\text{day count}}$$

OPTIONS

Standard deviation

$$\text{standard deviation} = \sqrt{\frac{\sum_{t=1}^{n}(\text{return at time } t - \text{mean return})^2}{\text{number of observations} - 1}}$$

Calculating the volatility over a period from annualised volatility

volatility over period t = annualised volatility $\sqrt{t}$

Where t is in years or fractions thereof.

A. USD 124,641,442.43
B. USD 124,636,476.94
C. USD 124,635,416.67
D. USD 123,915,737.30

Correct Answer: B Section: Volume F

QUESTION 340
What is the day count/annual basis convention for euroyen deposits?

A. Actual/365
B. Actual/360
C. Actual/actual
D. 30E/360

Correct Answer: B Section: Volume F

QUESTION 341
Which of the following are transferable instruments?

A. Eurocertificate of deposit
B. US Treasury bill
C. CP
D. All of the above

Correct Answer: D Section: Volume F

QUESTION 342
Which of the following is sometimes called two-name paper?

A. ECP
B. BA or bank bill
C. Treasury bill
D. CD

Correct Answer: B Section: Volume F

QUESTION 343
What usually happens to the collateral in a tri-party repo?

A. It is put at the disposal of the buyer
B. It is held by the seller in the name of the buyer
C. It is held by the tn-party agent in the name of the buyer
D. It is frozen in the sellers account with the tri-panty agent

Correct Answer: C Section: Volume F

QUESTION 344
Which type of repo is the least risky for the buyer?

A. Delivery repo
B. HIC repo
C. Tri-party repo
D. There is no real difference

Correct Answer: A Section: Volume F

QUESTION 345
The one-month (31-day) GC repo rate for French government bonds is quoted to you at 3.75-80%. As collateral, you are offered EUR25 million nominal of the 5.5% OAT April 2006, which is worth EUR 28,137,500. If you impose an initial margin of 1%, the Repurchase Price is:

A. EUR 27,947,276.43
B. EUR 27,946,077.08
C. EUR 27,950,071.43
D. EUR 27,948,871.97

Correct Answer: D Section: Volume F

QUESTION 346
If EUR/USD is quoted to you as 1.1050-53, does this price represent?

A. The number of EUP per USD
B. The number of USD per EUR
C. Depends on whether the price is being quoted in Europe or the US
D. Depends on whether the price is being quoted interbank or to a customer

Correct Answer: B Section: Volume F

QUESTION 347
How much is a big figure worth per million of base currency it EUR/GBP is 0.6990?

A. GBP 10,000
B. EUR 10,000
C. GBP 6,990
D. EUR 6,990

Correct Answer: A Section: Volume F

QUESTION 348
What is the incentive for market-making?

A. Bid/offer spread
B. Flow information
C. Relationships
D. All of the above

Correct Answer: D Section: Volume F

QUESTION 349
The torward points are calculated from:

A. The level of interest rates in the base currency
B. The level of interest rates in the quoted currency
C. The interest rates in the two currencies
D. Your expectations of the future spot rate

Correct Answer: C Section: Volume F

QUESTION 350
If 6-month EUR/AUD is quoted at 29/32, which of the following statements is correct?

A. EUR rates are higher than AUD rates in the 6-month
B. AUD rates are higher than EUR rates in the 6-month
C. There is a positive EUR yield curie
D. There is not enough information to decide

Correct Answer: B Section: Volume F

QUESTION 351
The Interest Rate Parity Theorem states that:

A. Interest rates in different currencies will tend to move into line with each other over time
B. Interest rates in different currencies differ due to differences in expectations about inflation
C. Selling a low interest rate currency to invest a high interest rate currency will only be profitable if one hedges the currency risk
D. Selling a low interest rate currency to invest in a high interest rate currency should not be profitable if one hedges the currency risk

Correct Answer: D Section: Volume F

QUESTION 352
What is an FX swap?

A. An exchange ot two streams of interest payments in different currencies and an exchange of the principal amounts of those currencies at maturity
B. A spot sale (purchase) and a forward purchase (sale) of two currencies agreed simultaneously between two parties
C. An exchange of currencies on a date beyond spot and at a price fixed today
D. None of the above

Correct Answer: B Section: Volume F

QUESTION 353
If I say that I have "bought and sold" EUR/USD in an FX swap, what have I done?

A. Bought EUR and sold USD spot, and sold FUR and bought USD forward
B. Bought EUR/USD spot and sold EUR/USD forward
C. Taken a EUR loan in exchange for making a USD loan with the same counterparly
D. All of the above

Correct Answer: D Section: Volume F

QUESTION 354
The mid-rate for USD/CHF is 1.3950 and the mid-rate for AUD/USD is 0.7060. What is the midrate for CHF/AUD?

A. 0.9849
B. 1.0154
C. 1.9759
D. 0.5061

Correct Answer: A Section: Volume F

QUESTION 355
Click on the Exhibit Button to view the Formula Sheet, If GBP/USD is

1.5350-53 and USD/JPY is 106.50-53, what is GBP/JPY? A. 163.48-56

B. 163.51-52
C. 69.36-39
D. 69.36-39

Correct Answer: A Section: Volume F

QUESTION 356
If spot GBP/CHF is quoted 2.3875-80 and the 3-month forward outright is 2.3660-70, what are the forward points?

A. 21.5/21
B. 210/215
C. 215/210
D. 21/21.5
Correct Answer: C Section: Volume F

QUESTION 357
Your are quoted the following rates:
spot CHF/JPY 60.12-22 3M CHF/JPY 25.5/22.5
At what rate can you buy 3-month outright JPY against CHF?

A. 79.995
B. 79.965
C. 79.895
D. 79.865
Correct Answer: D Section: Volume F

QUESTION 358
You are quoted the following market rates:

Spot USD/JPY 123.65 1M (30-day) USD. 2.15%
1M (30-day)JPY 0.10%

What is 1-month USD/JPY? A. 123.44
B. 123.65
C. 123.86
D. 123.90

Correct Answer: A Section: Volume F

QUESTION 359
A forward-forward loan creates an exposure to the risk of:

A. Higher interest rates
B. Lower interest rates
C. Steepening yield curve
D. Parallel shift downwards in the yield curve

Correct Answer: A Section: Volume F

QUESTION 360
You have a USD loan that is priced at 3-month LIBOR+50. LIBOR for the loan will be re-fixed in exactly one month. The market is quoting:

1x3 USD FRA. 1.95-98%
1x4 USD FRA. 2.07-10%
1x6 USD FRA 2.25-28%

To hedge the next LIBOR fixing, you should:

A. Sell a 1x3 FRA at 1.95%
B. Buy a 1x3 FRA at 1.98%
C. Buy a 1x4 FRA at 2.10%
D. Sell a 1x4 FRA at 2.10%

Correct Answer: C Section: Volume F

QUESTION 361
You bought a USD 4,000000 6x9 FRA at 6.75%. The settlement rate is 3-month (90-day) BBA LIBOR, which is fixed at 5.50%. What is the settlement amount at maturity?

A. You receive USD 12,330.46
B. You pay USD 12,330.46
C. You pay USD 12,163.81
D. You receive USD 12,163.81

Correct Answer: B Section: Volume F

QUESTION 362
The major difference between futures and OTC instruments like FRAs and interest rate swaps is that futures are:

A. Exchange-traded
B. Guaranteed
C. Standardised
D. All of the above

Correct Answer: D Section: Volume F

QUESTION 363
You are paying 5% per annum paid semi-annually and receiving 6-month LIBOR on a USD 10 million interest rate swap with exactly two years to maturity. 6-month LIBOR for the next payment date is fixed today at 4.95%. You expect 6-month LIBOR in 6 months to fix at 5.25%, in 12 months at 5.35% and in 18 months at 5.40%. What do you expect the net settlement amounts to be over the next 2 years? Assume 30-day months.

A. pay 250, receive 1,250, receive 1,750, receive 2,000
B. receive 250, pay 1,250, pay 1,750, pay 2,000
C. pay 2,500, receive 12,500, receive 17,500, receive 20,000
D. receive 2,500, pay 12,500, pay 17,500, pay 20,000

Correct Answer: C Section: Volume F

QUESTION 364
The intrinsic value of a long call option:

A. Falls and rises with the price of the underlying commodity, but is always positive
B. Rises if the price of the underlying commodity falls and vice versa

C. Depends solely on the volatility of the price of the underlying commodity
D. Becomes negative if the market price of the underlying commodity falls below the strike price of the option

Correct Answer: A Section: Volume F

QUESTION 365
What is the probability of an at-the-money option being exercised?

A. Less than 50% probability
B. 50% probability
C. More than 50% probability
D. Zero probability

Correct Answer: B Section: Volume F

QUESTION 366
A dealer does the following deals in EUR/USD:

buys EUR 1 m at 11020
sells EUR 3 m at 1.1022
buys EUR 2 m at 1.1002
buys EUR 1.5 m at 1.1012

What position does the dealer now have?

A. Long EUR 1.5 m at 1.0984
B. Short EUP 1.5 m at 1.1036
C. Long EUR 1.5 m at 1.1012
D. Short EUR 3.0 mat 1.1025

Correct Answer: A Section: Volume F

QUESTION 367
Fraud is typically classified as:

A. Credit risk
B. Market risk
C. Legal risk
D. Operational risk

Correct Answer: D Section: Volume F

QUESTION 368
What is the effect of netting?

A. To reduce the number and size of payments and transfers
B. To reduce exposure to credit risk
C. To reduce the size of the balance sheet
D. All of the above

Correct Answer: D
Section: Volume F

QUESTION 369
What is a Vostro account?

A. Your account at another bank
B. A foreign bank's account in your bank in your domestic currency
C. An account in your bank used for internal transactions
D. A customer's account at your bank

Correct Answer: B Section: Volume F

QUESTION 370
For which of the following reasons is the extension of forward contracts at non-current rates is discouraged:

i. These could be used to conceal profit or losses.
ii. These could be used to perpetrate fraud.
iii. These could result in an unauthorised extension of credit.
iv. These could result in confusing settlement instructions.

A. (i), (ii), (iii), & (iv).
B. (i), (ii) & (iii).
C. (i) & (iii).
D. none of the above.

Correct Answer: B Section: Volume F

QUESTION 371
Confirmations must be sent out

A. Immediately after the deal is done.
B. As quickly as possible after the deal is done.
C. By electronic media only, e.g. fax, telex.
D. Not later than the value date of the first leg of the transaction.

Correct Answer: B Section: Volume F

QUESTION 372
Where the matter of dealing for personal account is concerned, the Model Code recommends that

A. Subject to local legal requirements, this matter is one for bank management to decide.
B. Bank management should encourage such activities because it allows banks to monitor the gambling habits of their staff.
C. Where this is allowed, bank management should have a clearly defined policy and written procedures.
D. Bank management should allow staff to deal for their personal account on a case to case basis.

Correct Answer: C Section: Volume F

QUESTION 373
To curb attempted fraud, banks should:

A. Require greater vigilance by the management and staff.
B. Take particular care when the beneficiary is a third party to the deal.
C. Ensure that details of all telephone deals which do not include pre-agreed standard settlement instructions are confirmed by telex or similar means without delay.
D. All of the above.

Correct Answer: D Section: Volume F

QUESTION 374
Written confirmation is a function that can be done by:

A. Any dealer as long as he/she is not a party to the trade.
B. Staff in the back-office.
C. Staff in the dealing room who are not dealing.
D. Any staff outside the dealing room.

Correct Answer: B Section: Volume F

QUESTION 375
Which of following is not true?

A. Inter-bank market participants have a duty to make absolutely clear whether the prices they are quoting are firm or merely indicative.
B. It is the duty of the dealer to periodically confirm with the broker the validity of his price.
C. It is the responsibility of the dealer to ensure that prices given to a broker are taken off if they have not been hit or were subject to a time limit.
D. No deal is done if one counterparty is unable to conclude a deal due to credit line problems and a name switch is not found within a reasonable period of time.

Correct Answer: B Section: Volume F

QUESTION 376
Which of the following statements is true?

A. Banks should not ask brokers to disclose details of third party transactions unless they are between overseas principals.
B. Banks should not ask brokers to disclose details of third party transactions unless these transactions are already settled.
C. Banks should not ask brokers to disclose transactions between third parties in any circumstances.
D. Banks should not ask brokers for details of third party transactions unless senior management has approved.

Correct Answer: C Section: Volume F

QUESTION 377
Click on the Exhibit Button to view the Formula Sheet. Bank A pays for EURO 5 m at 1.1592. Bank B offers EURO 10 m at 1.1597. Broker XYZ quotes to the market EURO /USD 1.1592/97. Bank C takes the offer at 97. The broker is obliged to reveal:

A. The name of Banks A and B.
B. The name of Bank B only.
C. The amount that was bid but not the name of Bank A.
D. None of the above

Correct Answer: B Section: Volume F

QUESTION 378
When you are accepting a stop loss order, you must:

A. Ensure that your counterparty understands the terms under which your bank accepts the order.
B. Ensure that your counterpart can be contacted in the event of unusual situations or events or extremely volatile market conditions.
C. Ensure that your counterparty understands that any guarantee or fixed price execution requires agreement in writing.
D. All of the above.

Correct Answer: C Section: Volume F

QUESTION 379
Brokers shall not reveal the identity of a counterparty unless:

A. They are forced to do so.
B. Explicitly authorised to do so by the counterparty.
C. They know the counterparty very well.
D. They are asked by their senior management to do so.

Correct Answer: B Section: Volume F

QUESTION 380
Which of the following statements reflects the Model Code on gambling or betting amongst market participants?

A. Gambling and betting between market participants should be strongly discouraged.
B. Gambling and betting between market participants can be allowed if it is monitored by management.
C. Gambling and betting between market participants should be forbidden.
D. All of the above.

Correct Answer: A Section: Volume F

QUESTION 381
Where answer phone equipment is used for reporting and recording of off-premises transactions, it should be:

A. On an special number known only to the chief dealer.
B. On a number located in the office of the internal auditor.
C. Secured so that reported transactions cannot be erased without senior management approval.
D. Secured by recordings that are stored for a suitable period.

Correct Answer: C Section: Volume F

QUESTION 382
When quoting the exchange rate between the EUR and AUDI which is conventionally the base currency?

A. EUR
B. AUD
C. Depends on whether the price is being quoted in Europe or Australia
D. Depends on whether the price is being quoted interbank or to a customer

Correct Answer: A Section: Volume G

QUESTION 383
Are the forward points materially affected by changes in the spot rate?

A. never
B. Only for very large movements and longer terms
C. always
D. spot is the principal influence

Correct Answer: B Section: Volume G

QUESTION 384
A 6-month SEK/NOK Swap is quoted 140/150. Spot is 0.9445. Which of the following statements is correct?

A. SEK interest rates are higher than NOK interest rates
B. NOK interest rates are higher than SEK interest rates
C. NOK interest rates are higher than USD interest rates
D. SEK interest rates and NOK interest rates are converging

Correct Answer: B Section: Volume G

QUESTION 385
How is an outright forward FX transaction quoted?

A. Forward points
B. Full forward exchange rate
C. Depends on whether is interbank or to a customer
D. Depends on the currency pair and sometimes the term

Correct Answer: B Section: Volume G

QUESTION 386
Spot cable is quoted at 1.6048-53 in the brokers and you quote a customer 1.6050-55 in USD 3 million, If they sell USD to you, how much GSP will you be short of?

A. 4,816,500.00
B. 1,868,809.57
C. 1.868,576.77
D. 4,815,900.00

Correct Answer: C Section: Volume G

QUESTION 387
If spot AUD/USD is quoted to you as 0.7406-09. How many AUD would you receive in exchange for USD 5,000,000 if you dealt on the price?

A. 3,704,500
B. 6,748,549
C. 3,703,000
D. 6,751,283

Correct Answer: B Section: Volume G

QUESTION 388
If GSP/USD is quoted to you at 1.61 20-30, how much GSP would you receive if you sold USD 2000,000?

A. 1,239,925.60
B. 1,237,873.80
C. 1,240,694.79
D. 1,242,720.50

Correct Answer: A Section: Volume G

QUESTION 389
If EUR/USD is 1.1025-28 and the 6-month swap is 112.50/113, what is the 6-month outright price?

A. 1.1380-1.11405
B. 1.11375-1.1141
C. 1.09125-1.0915
D. None of these

Correct Answer: B Section: Volume G

QUESTION 390
You quote the following rates to a customer spot GBP/CHF 2.2005-10 3M GBP/CHF swap 120/115

At what rate do you sell GBP to a customer 3-month outright? A. 2.1890
B. 2.2125
C. 2.1895
D. 2.1885

Correct Answer: C Section: Volume G

QUESTION 391
Lending for 3 months and borrowing for 6 months creates a 3x6 forward-forward deposit. The cost of that deposit is called:

A. Break-even rate
B. Implied rate
C. Forward-forward rate
D. All of the above

Correct Answer: D Section: Volume G

QUESTION 392
Today is Monday, 8th December. You sell a 9x12 FRA for value Thursday, 10th September next year. On what date is the settlement amount due to be paid or received (assuming that there are no holidays)?

A. 8th September next year
B. 10th September next year
C. 8th December next year
D. 10th December next year

Correct Answer: B Section: Volume G

QUESTION 393
Click on the Exhibit Button to view the Formula Sheet. You are short of 6 Dec euro dollar futures contracts at 98.10. Yesterday, the closing price was 98.15. Today's closing price is 97.905.Whatvariation margin will be due?

A. You will have to pay USD 612.50
B. You will receive USD 612.50
C. You will have to pay USD 3,675.00
D. You will receive USD 3,675.00
Correct Answer: D Section: Volume G

QUESTION 394
Which of the following is true?

A. The CME eurodollar futures contract has a tick value (for one full basis point equivalent) of USD25 and a face value of USD 1,000,000
B. The Euronext. LIFFE EURIBOR futures contract has a tick value (for one full basis point equivalent) of EUR25 and a face value of EUR 1,000,000
C. The Euronext.LIFFE CHF futures contract has a tick value (for one full basis point equivalent) of CHF25 and a face value of CHF 1,000,000
D. All of the above

Correct Answer: D Section: Volume G

QUESTION 395
You are paying 5% per annum paid semi-annually and receiving 6-month LIBOR on a USD 10 million interest rate swap with exactly two years to maturity. 6-month LIBOR for the next payment date is fixed today at 4.95%. How would you hedge the swap using FRAs? How to hedge an IRS with a strip of FRAs?

A. buy a strip of 0x6, 6x12, 12x18 and 18x24 FRAs
B. sell a strip of 0x6, 6x12, 12x18 and 18x24 FRAs
C. buy a strip of 6x12, 12x10 and 16x24 FRAs
D. sell a strip of 6x12, 12x18 and 18x24 FRAs

Correct Answer: D Section: Volume G

QUESTION 396
The premium on an option contract is:

A. The price of the underlying commodity at the time of the transaction
B. The price at which the transaction on the underlying commodity will be carried out if and when the option is exercised
C. The price the buyer of the option pays to the seller when entering into the options contract
D. The price at which the two counterparties can close-out their position

Correct Answer: C Section: Volume G

QUESTION 397
The delta of an at-the-money long call option is:

A. Between +0.5 and +1
B. +0.5
C. Between 0 and +0.5
D. Zero

Correct Answer: B Section: Volume G

QUESTION 398
You bought USD 5,000,000 against EUR at 1.1037 and 3,000,000 at 1.1052. If the EUR/USD rate is now quoted 1.1015/17, and it you deal at that rate, what profitwould you make?

A. Nil
B. A profit of EUR 16,847.58
C. A loss
D. A profit of EUR 18,166.05

Correct Answer: B Section: Volume G

QUESTION 399
A disgruntled customer claims that he should not have to settle an FRA with you because it is really just a wager. What type of risk are you exposed to?

A. Credit risk
B. Legal risk
C. Settlement risk
D. Basis risk

Correct Answer: B Section: Volume G

QUESTION 400
Which of the following is not true?

A. The Model Code is published by ACI's Committee for Professionalism.
B. The Model Code sets out the practicalities of dealing in those financial instruments listed in the Model Code.
C. The Model Code is an attempt to deal with the legal issues relating to every conceivable financialinstrument.
D. The Model Code sets out the manner and spirit in which foreign

exchange and money market business should be conducted in order that participants maintain high standards of professionalism, integrity and ethical conduct.

Correct Answer: C Section: Volume G

QUESTION 401
In spite of having agreed to a deal, dealers are not bound to the deal if it is subject to documentation. The Model Code:

A. Does not regard this as a good practice.
B. Urge dealers to be bear this in mind, as this is common practice for capital market deals.
C. Does not comment on this matter.
D. Recommends that national ACI Associations deal with this according to their local customs.

Correct Answer: A Section: Volume G

QUESTION 402
Bank B's price is shown by a broker to Bank A and is dealt by Bank A. If Bank A wants to increase the amount of the transaction, what is good market practice according to the Model Code:

A. Bank A can call Bank B directly.
B. Bank A should wait 10 minutes before calling Bank B.
C. Bank A cannot increase the amount.
D. Bank A should go back to the broker.

Correct Answer: D Section: Volume G

QUESTION 403
The use of standard settlement instructions (SSI's) is strongly encouraged because:

A. It reduces operational risk.
B. It splits differences arising from failed settlement between the two counterparties.
C. It removes the need for sending out SWIFT payment authorisations.
D. All of the above.

Correct Answer: A Section: Volume G

QUESTION 404
Under which circumstances are banks allowed to park positions with a counterparty?:

A. It is forbidden to park positions.
B. In conditions of exceptional volatility.
C. If the two counterparties agree.
D. If approved by senior management.

Correct Answer: A Section: Volume G

QUESTION 405
In a dispute between the dealer and a broker, the Model Code recommends that this should be referred in the first instance to:

A. Central bank.
B. Senior management of the bank and the brokerage firm.
C. Head of compliance.
D. ACI's Committee for Professionalism (CFP).

Correct Answer: B Section: Volume G

QUESTION 406
The term "under reference" refers to:

A. An unavailability of credit limit for the counterparty.
B. The need to reconfirm a transaction.
C. The unacceptability of the counterparty's name.
D. The rate quoted is going to be revised.

Correct Answer: B Section: Volume G

QUESTION 407
When a broker calls "off" at the very instant a dealer "hits" the broker's price:

A. The transaction should be concluded.
B. The broker decides whether or not the deal is done.
C. ACI's Committee for Professionalism will decide whether the transaction should be concluded.
D. The transaction should not be concluded.

Correct Answer: D Section: Volume G

QUESTION 408
If a dealer has interest on one side, and the other side is dealt away, the broker should:

A. Immediately put the price "under reference" and check with the dealer to ascertain his original intention.
B. Cancel the order.
C. Continue with the order.
D. None of the above.

Correct Answer: A Section: Volume G

QUESTION 409
Bank XYZ calls you for a quote in EUR/USD for EURO 20 million. If you decide to quote to Bank XYZ:

A. You must be prepared to deal up to EUR 20 million.
B. You may quote without stating the amount you are prepared to deal.
C. You are only committed to deal in a marketable amount.
D. None or the above.

Correct Answer: A Section: Volume G

QUESTION 410
The use of mobile phones within the dealing room is not considered good practice except

A. In volatile markets.
B. When dealing with emerging markets.
C. In an emergency.
D. When quoting for information only.

Correct Answer: C Section: Volume G

QUESTION 411
The organisational structure of market participants should ensure a strict segregation between front and back office of:

A. Duties and reporting lines.
B. Systems.
C. Career paths.
D. All of the above.

Correct Answer: A Section: Volume G

QUESTION 412
The Chairman and members of the ACIs Committee for Professionalism are ready to assist in resolving disputes through the ACIs Expert Determination Service in situations where:

A. The amount of the deal exceeds EUR 5 million.
B. The local regulator or central bank declines to intervene.
C. Litigation has already commenced.
D. At the request of one of the counterparties.

Correct Answer: D Section: Volume G

QUESTION 413
Where the Committee for Professionalism of the ACI has been notified of a breach of the letter or spirit of the Model Code, it

A. Will examine the complaint.
B. May consult with the local ACI.
C. Will bring the matter to the attention of the local regulator.
D. None of the above.

Correct Answer: A Section: Volume G

QUESTION 414
Where repos or securities lending transactions are entered into, the Model Code recommends:

A. Documentation should be in place beforehand.
B. Management should approve all transactions.
C. Copies of the underlying documentation should be lodged with regulators.
D. All of the above.

Correct Answer: A Section: Volume G

QUESTION 415
Where internet trading facilities are established by a bank for a client, the conditions and controls should be stated in a rulebook produced by:

A. The bank.
B. The local bankers association.
C. The local regulator.
D. Negotiation between the bank and client.

Correct Answer: A Section: Volume G

QUESTION 416
You and a dealer at another bank have an informal bilateral reciprocal arrangement to quote each other two-way prices. During periods of high volatility, the other dealer refuses to quote to you. The Model Code states that

A. The other dealer should act with honour, honesty and integrity.
B. It is a purely matter for your two institutions.
C. Such arrangements are not in any way enforceable or binding.
D. All of the above.

Correct Answer: B Section: Volume G

QUESTION 417
Management policy on the use of mobile devices by trading sales and settlement staff should:

A. Ban them from the dealing room or back office.
B. State whether they are allowed in the dealing room and back office, and can be used.
C. Ban their use in the dealing room or back office.
D. Restrict their use to senior management and authorised out-of-hours trading and sales staff.

Correct Answer: B Section: Volume G

QUESTION 418
When dealing with a fund manager, who will allocate shares in a transaction to his unknown clients after the transaction has been executed with you, you should:

A. Agree in writing with the fund manager that the allocation will be confirmed as soon as practicable after the transaction is executed.
B. Insist on the allocation being made and confirmed before the transaction is executed.
C. Agree in writing with the fund manager that he will guarantee the transaction until the allocation is confirmed.
D. Any of the above.

Correct Answer: A Section: Volume G

QUESTION 419
What is the risk of dealing through an agent with an unknown principal?

A. You may not be able to ensure that your firm can avoid suspicion of trading on non-public information or other allegations of bad or illegal trading practice.
B. You may not be able to net your exposure in an insolvency.
C. You may not be able to net your exposure for capital adequacy purposes.
D. All of the above.

Correct Answer: D Section: Volume G

QUESTION 420
Which of the following currencies is quoted on an actual/360 basis?

A. EUR
B. JPY
C. CHF
D. All of the above

Correct Answer: D Section: Volume G

QUESTION 421
When is interest conventionally due on a 3-year interbank eurodollar deposit?

A. At maturity
B. Annually
C. Semi-annually
D. Quarterly

Correct Answer: B Section: Volume G

QUESTION 422
Today's date is Thursday 12th December. What is the spot value date? Assume no bank holidays.

A. 14th December
B. 15th December
C. 16th December
D. 17th December

Correct Answer: C Section: Volume G

QUESTION 423
From the following GBP deposit rates:

1M (31-day) GBP deposits 3.15% 2M (61-day) GBP deposits 3.25% 3M (91-day) GBP deposits 3.41% 4M (120-day) GBP deposits 3.56% 5M (152-day) GBP deposits 3.73% 6M (182-day) GBP deposits 3.90%

calculate the 3x4 forward-forward rate. A. 3.410%

B. 3.977%
C. 3.996%
D. 3.997%

Correct Answer: D Section: Volume G

QUESTION 424
Which of the following are quoted in terms of a yield-to-maturity?

A. USCP
B. ECP
C. Treasury bill
D. BA

Correct Answer: B Section: Volume G

QUESTION 425
What is the buyers primary risk in a repo?

A. The credit risk on the collateral
B. The credit risk on the repo counterparty
C. The legal risk on the contract
D. The operational risk on margin maintenance

Correct Answer: B Section: Volume G

QUESTION 426
How can material divergences between the value of cash and collateral be managed in a documented sell/buy-back?

A. Margin maintenance
B. Re-pricing
C. Either of the above, but usually (a)
D. Either of the above, but usually (b)

Correct Answer: D Section: Volume G

QUESTION 427
The two-week repo rate br the 5.25% bund 2007 is quoted to you at 3.33-38%. You agree to reverse in bonds worth EUR 266,125,000 with no initial margin. You would earn repo interest ot

A. EUR 349,806
B. EUR 344,632
C. EUR 319,315
D. EUR 324,110

Correct Answer: B Section: Volume G

QUESTION 428
What is the ISO code for the Lebanon pound?

A. LEP
B. LBD
C. LBP
D. LNP

Correct Answer: C Section: Volume G

QUESTION 429
A dealer needs to buy USD against SGD. Of the following rates quoted to him, which is the best rate for him?

A. 1.4323-26
B. 1.4320-25
C. 1.4315-20
D. 1.4318-23

Correct Answer: C Section: Volume G

QUESTION 430
You need to buy USD 5,000,000 against GBP and are quoted the following rates concurrently by two separate banks: 1.6045-50 and 1.6047-52. At which rate do you trade?

A. 1.6045
B. 1.6047
C. 1.6050
D. 1.6052

Correct Answer: B Section: Volume G

QUESTION 431
Cable is quoted at 1.6075-80 and you say "5 yours!" to the broker. What have you done?

A. Sold USD 5 million at 1.6075
B. Sold GBP 5 million at 1.6075
C. Bought GBP 5 million at 1.60B0
D. Bought USD 5 million at 1.6080

Correct Answer: B Section: Volume G

QUESTION 432
You are quoted spot NZD/USD 0.6821-26 and USD/CHF 1.4652-56 at what price can you buy CHF against NZD?

A. 0.9993
B. 1.0006
C. 1.0007
D. 0.9994

Correct Answer: D Section: Volume G

QUESTION 433
You have quoted a Swiss customer spot USD/CHF as 1.3710-15, but he asks you to quote it as CHF/USD. What do you quote?

A. 0.7291-94
B. 0.7294-91
C. 1.3710-15
D. None of these

Correct Answer: A Section: Volume G

QUESTION 434
You are quoted the following market rates:

spot EUR/CHF 1.1005 6M (180-day) EUR 3.45%
6M (180-day) CHF 1.25%

What are the 6-month EUR/CHF forward points? A. +121
B. +120
C. -116
D. -119

Correct Answer: D Section: Volume G

QUESTION 435
Using the following rates:

spot GBP/CHF 2.3785-15
spot CHF/SEK 5.5975-85 3M GBP/SEK swap 725/690

What is the price for 3-month outright GBP/SEK? A. 13.3860-13.4020
B. 13.2435-13.2615
C. 13.2412-13.2638
D. 13.2445-13.2605

Correct Answer: C Section: Volume G

QUESTION 436
The market is quoting:

1-month (31-day) USD. 1.75% 3-month (91-day) USD. 2.05%

What is the 1x3 rate in USD? A. 4.261%
B. 2.202%
C. 1.900%
D. 1.592%

Correct Answer: B Section: Volume G

QUESTION 437
A customer sells a LIFFE Euro Swiss futures contract. Which of the following risks could he be trying to hedge?

A. An increase in forward USD/CHF
B. Falling CHF interest rates
C. A decrease in forward USD/CHF
D. Rising CHF interest rates

Correct Answer: D Section: Volume G

QUESTION 438
Purchasing a USD/JPY call option is equivalent to:

A. Selling an JPY/USD put option
B. Selling a JPY/USD call option
C. Purchasing an JPY/USD put option
D. None of the above

Correct Answer: C Section: Volume G

QUESTION 439
An option premium is a positive function of:

A. Time to expiry
B. The volatility of the price of the underlying commodity
C. The moneyness of the option
D. All of the above

Correct Answer: D Section: Volume G

QUESTION 440
The delta of an option is:

A. The sensitivity of the option value to changes in interest rates
B. The sensitivity of the option value to changes in volatility
C. The sensitivity of the option value to changes in the time to expiry
D. The sensitivity of the option value to changes in the price of the underlying

Correct Answer: D Section: Volume G

QUESTION 441
What is the purpose of a long strangle option strategy?

A. To anticipate very low volatility in the price of the underlying commodity
B. To anticipate moderately high volatility in the price of the underlying commodity
C. To anticipate moderate volatility in the price of the underlying commodity
D. To anticipate very high volatility in the price of the underlying commodity

Correct Answer: D Section: Volume G

QUESTION 442
If you buy GBP 2,000,000 against USD at 1.6020; GSP 1,000,000 at 1.6035 and GBP 3,000,000 at 1.6028, what is the average rate of your position?

A. 1.6035
B. 1.6027
C. 1.6030
D. 1.6023

Correct Answer: B Section: Volume G

QUESTION 443
What is replacement cost a function of?

A. Credit risk
B. Market risk
C. Both of the above
D. None of the above

Correct Answer: A Section: Volume G

QUESTION 444
What is a master agreement intended to do?

A. Describe the parameters of a dealing relationship
B. Set out the rights and obligations of two parties
C. Apply to all transactions between two parties
D. All of the above

Correct Answer: D Section: Volume G

www.ingramcontent.com/pod-product-compliance
Lightning Source LLC
Chambersburg PA
CBHW050005230526
45465CB00003BB/1270